LEARNING 300 CHINESE PROVERBS

TALK THE WISDOM

Susan Zhi Chang & Peter T. Treadway

Audio file in MP3 format downloadable via website

Pinyin and four tones above every Chinese character

Order this book online at www.trafford.com
or email orders@trafford.com

Most Trafford titles are also available at major online book retailers.

Printed in the United States of America.

ISBN: 978-1-4269-6303-2 (sc)
ISBN: 978-1-4669-0277-0 (e)

Library of Congress Control Number: 2011960019

Trafford rev. 05/25/2012

www.trafford.com

North America & international
toll-free: 1 888 232 4444 (USA & Canada)
phone: 250 383 6864 • fax: 812 355 4082

Preface

This is a book of Chinese proverbs. We think it is very unique. It is first and foremost a tool for learning spoken and written Mandarin Chinese, complete with sections on grammar and an innovative approach to learning pronunciation. In that sense, it is a very practical book, useful to the beginner and advanced student alike. Every proverb represents a new lesson. Students can choose whatever proverb interests them at a given moment.

The book may be of use not only to English-speaking students of Chinese but also to native Chinese speakers who want to learn more about English as well as their own language. The book uses Simplified Chinese and the Pinyin transliteration system for rendering Chinese characters into English. Both of these are the standards used in Mainland China. China has many spoken dialects, but the pronunciation followed in these books is that of standard Mandarin.

The book is much more than a Chinese textbook. China has a civilization and language that go back thousands of years. Buddhism, Confucianism, Legalism, Daoism, an awareness of history, a sinocentric worldview, and yes, male chauvinism—all permeate the Chinese language. Chinese proverbs are, in a sense, the DNA of Chinese culture and language, blueprints preserving the past and advising the present. Speakers of Chinese know what these proverbs are saying, but Westerners need a guide. The meanings of many of the proverbs are not obvious to Westerners. For example, when Chinese say the proverb "Dog chases mouse," they mean "Mind your own business." (Dogs don't chase mice; it's not their job.) It is no wonder that English-speaking people can find Chinese difficult. The thought process is different.

The book is the product of two people working together, one a native Chinese artist (Susan) who has lived in the United States since 1981 and the other an American writer, money manager, and economist (Peter) who has lived in Asia for many years and who does not speak or write Chinese. The book is the product of two people of different backgrounds interchanging and mixing ideas, of two people actually fighting and screaming at one another until we got it right! Writing the book was great fun—and sheer torture.

Susan compiled the proverbs and did the initial translations. It was Peter's job to write a Comment for the proverbs and to put them all into flowing, not-always-literal, grammatically correct English. We did not want fortune cookie translations.

Susan also did the delightful sketches that can be found with many of the proverbs. One picture is worth a thousand words, and readers can immerse themselves in the Chinese atmosphere.

A proverb in Chinese must have more than four characters. If a saying has only four characters, it is an "idiom." This book is about proverbs only.

Also a note on gender: For the English translations and Comments, we have elected to use the traditional masculine "he" and "his" rather than the logical but clumsy "he or she" and "his or her" or the politically correct "she" and "her." This seemed more convenient since, although Chinese generally does not specify a gender at all, frequently the reference is in fact masculine. We hope the reader will understand this choice.

Finally, recordings of all the proverbs in Mandarin Chinese in MP3 format can be downloaded from www.susanchang.com/300audio.

Susan Zhi Chang

Peter T. Treadway, PhD

Contents

Preface 2-3

List of proverbs in Chinese 4-21

01．爱之欲其生，恶之欲其死。........ 22
Love somebody, wish him a long life; hate somebody, wish he would die.

02．百足之虫，死而不僵。........ 23
A hundred foot long bug is dead but it's still not stiff.

03．包子有肉不在褶上。........ 24
You can not tell how much meat the steamed buns have inside from the fold of the buns.

04．饱谙世事慵开眼，会尽人情只点头。........ 25
When something happens, a person who has a full understanding of the ways of the world will not bother to open his eyes; he only bows his head appearing to agree.

05．备他一顶轿，起他一个号，刻他一部稿，娶他一个小。........ 26
1) Prepare a sedan chair, 2) adopt an elegant pseudonym, 3) carve an article on wood and 4) get a young concubine.

06．被窝里放屁，糟蹋自己。........ 27
Spoil yourself by releasing gas under the blanket.

07．变戏法的瞒不过打锣的。........ 28
The person who performs the magic tricks cannot hide the secret from the person who beat the gong.

08．病急乱投医。........ 29
When very sick and in urgent need of help, see any doctor no matter good or bad.

09．不到西天不知佛大小。........ 30-31
If you don't reach the western paradise, you will not know how big the Buddha is.

10．捕得老鼠，打破油瓶。........ 32
One way to catch a mouse is to hit the cooking oil bottle; the mouse is caught, but the bottle is broken into bits.

11．不管黑猫白猫，能抓老鼠就是好猫。........ 33
No matter if the cat is black or white, if it can catch a mouse it is a good cat.

12．不见棺材不掉泪。........ 34
If you do not see the coffin, you won't cry.

13．不见兔子不撒鹰。........ 35
Until you see the rabbit, don't release the falcon.

14．不看僧面看佛面，不念鱼情念水情。........ 36
If you don't give a monk face, you should give Buddha face; if you don't give a fish face, you should give the water face.

15．不能留芳百世，也要遗臭万年。....................................37
If I can't leave a good name in history, then leave a bad name.

16．不怕贼偷，就怕贼惦记。....................................38
Don't be afraid of being robbed by a thief; just be afraid the thief will think about you all the time.

17．不求有功，但求无过。....................................39
Don't demand for credit; only wish that you didn't make a mistake.

18．不入虎穴，焉得虎子？....................................40
If you do not enter the tiger's den, how can you catch the baby tiger?

19．不孝有三，无后为大。....................................41
There are three things that show a man is devoted to his parents; among these, having a son is the most important.

20．不做贼，心不惊；不吃鱼，嘴不腥。....................................42
If you are not a thief, you will not be frightened; if you do not eat the fish, you will have no stinking smell in the mouth.

21．不做中人不做保，一生一世无烦恼。....................................43
Don't be a middle man or a guarantor and your whole life will be without trouble.

22．苍蝇不叮无缝的蛋。....................................44
A fly doesn't suck an egg with no crack.

23．曾经沧海难为水，除却巫山不是云。....................................45
Once you see the dark blue sea, no other water is water; once you see the Wu Mountain's cloud, no other cloud is a cloud.

24．朝中有人好做官。....................................46-47
If you have people in the government, it will be much easier to secure an official position.

25．吃饭少一口，睡觉不蒙首，老婆长得丑，保你活到九十九。.........48-49
When you eat a meal, have one bite less; when you are sleeping, don't cover up your head; when your wife is ugly, it is guaranteed you will live to be ninety-nine.

26．城门失火，殃及池鱼。....................................50-51
The door on the city wall is on fire, bringing disaster to the fish in the moat.

27．常走夜路必定遇见鬼。....................................52
If you always walk on the road late at night, you will be sure to meet a ghost.

28．成事不足，败事有余。....................................53
He has enough ability to damage things but not enough to accomplish things.

29．吃素碰到月大。....................................54
A person decides to eat vegetarian for a month; unfortunately this month has thirty one days.

30．吃人嘴短，拿人手软。....................................55
If you eat other people's food, your mouth is short; if you take something from people, your hand is soft.

31．赤脚的不怕穿鞋的。....................................56
Barefoot people are not afraid of people who wear shoes.

32. 初生牛犊不怕虎。........................57
A new born calf is not afraid of the tiger.

33. 丑媳妇迟早要见公婆。........................58-59
An ugly daughter-in-law has to meet her husband's parents sooner or later.

34. 从俭入奢易，从奢入俭难。........................60
Changing from a poor life style to one of luxury is easy; changing from a life of luxury to one of thrift is difficult.

35. 打人休打脸，骂人休揭短。........................61
When you hit someone, do not hit his face; when you yell at somebody, do not reveal his shortcomings.

36. 打狗要看主人面。........................62-63
Before you beat a dog, consider its master's face.

37. 打虎亲兄弟，上阵父子兵。........................64-65
To hunt for a tiger you should have blood brothers with you; to go into battle comrades should be father and son.

38. 打肿脸充胖子。........................66
Slap your face until it is swollen and then pretend you are fat.

39. 大事化小，小事化了。........................67
Reduce a big problem into a small problem; then make the small problem fade away.

40. 大树底下好乘凉。........................68
The shade of the big tree offers a cool place to relax.

41. 大水冲了龙王庙，一家人不认得一家人。........................69
Water floods the dragon's temple; people in the same family do not recognize each other.

42. 大鱼吃小鱼，小鱼吃虾米。........................70
Big fish eat small fish; small fish eat shrimp.

43. 当官的动动嘴，当兵的跑断腿。........................71
The official moves his lips to command; the soldier runs and breaks his leg.

44. 当局者迷，旁观者清。........................72-73
The chess players are confused; the spectators see the game better than the players.

45. 当家是个年轻郎，餐餐窝头心不凉。........................74
The master of the family is a young man; at every meal his wife eats Wo Tou and still is perfectly happy.

46. 当着和尚骂贼秃。........................75
In the presence of a monk, he shouts "baldheaded thief" at another person.

47. 敌强用智，敌弱用势。........................76
When the enemy is big and powerful, use wisdom to deal with them; when the enemy is weak, use power.

48. 雕塑匠不给神像叩头——知道老底。........................77
The sculptor doesn't kowtow to the sculpture of the deity because he knows the inside story.

49. 爹有不如娘有，娘有不如老婆有，老婆有还要开开口，不如自己有。....78
When man's father has the money it is not as good as his mother; when the mother has it, it's not as good as his wife having it; he still has to open his mouth to ask his wife for it; better to have the money himself.

50. 丢了拐杖就受狗气。..79
Once you throw down your stick, you are going to be bullied by a dog.

51. 洞房花烛夜，金榜题名时。..................................80-81
The pleasures of the wedding night and the moment of the yellow color board's announcement of who succeeded in the government examination.

52. 对客不得嗔狗。..82
In front of guests you should not berate the dog.

53. 多年的小道流成河，多年的媳妇熬成婆。..........................83
For many years a small stream flows in a narrow path and then becomes a river; a daughter-in-law is tortured many years by her mother-in-law, but sooner or later she will become a mother-in-law.

54. 多情者必好色，好色者未必多情。................................84
If a man has a lot of love, he definitely will be full of lust. But a man who has lust may not necessarily have love.

55. 儿不嫌母丑，狗不嫌家贫。....................................85
A son never deserts his mother because of her ugly face; a dog won't forsake his master because the master is poor.

56. 儿孙自有儿孙福，莫为儿孙当马牛。..............................86
Later generations have their own fortune; don't become a horse and cow for them.

67. 法场上的麻雀，胆子早吓大了。..................................87
The sparrows who live in the execution grounds have more courage because they have been scared before.

58. 翻手为云，覆手为雨。..88
Turn the palm up, a cloud comes out; turn the palm down, a cloud becomes rain.

59. 放下屠刀，立地成佛。..89
A butcher immediately becomes a Buddha when he drops his cleaver.

60. 飞鸟尽，良弓藏；狡兔死，走狗烹；敌国破，谋臣亡。............90-91
When the birds are all killed, hide the excellent bow; when the rabbits are all dead, cook the hunting dog; when the enemy country has been defeated, execute the wartime officials.

61. 肥水不流外人田。..92
Manure shouldn't go to other people's land.

62. 风马牛不相及。..93
There is no sexual interest between a horse and a cow.

63. 父母在，不远游，游必有方。....................................94
When your parents are still alive, do not take a long trip; if you have to go, you must tell your parents where you are going.

64．富不过三代。..........95
Wealth cannot last three generations.

65．覆巢之下，岂有完卵。..........96
If the nest is turned upside down, how can you find unbroken eggs.

66．隔年的黄历不管用。..........97
Last year's imperial calendar is useless.

67．隔着布袋买猫。..........98
Buy a cat with the cat wrapped in a cotton bag.

68．恭敬莫如从命，受训莫如从顺。..........99
Politeness is not as good as obedience; being scolded is not as good as being respectful and submissive.

69．关公面前舞大刀。..........100-101
Wave a big knife in front of Guan Gong.

70．狗瘦莫踢，马病莫骑，人穷莫欺。..........102
Don't kick a thin dog; don't ride a sick horse; don't insult poor people.

71．挂羊头卖狗肉。..........103
Displays a sheep's head, but sells dog meat.

72．棺材里伸出手来——死要钱。..........104
The hand sticks out from the coffin, still desperate for money.

73．贵易交，富易妻。..........105
Become wealthy and achieve a higher social position; then get rid of old friends and old wife.

74．过河拆桥，卸磨杀驴。..........106
Dismantle a bridge right after crossing the river; kill the donkey right after unloading the millstone.

75．好马不吃回头草。..........107
A good horse will not turn back to eat the grass he just passed by.

76．好男不吃分家饭，好女不穿嫁时衣。..........108
A good son will not make a living by dividing up his family's property; a good daughter will not wear wedding clothes.

77．好男不与女斗，好狗不与鸡斗。..........109
A good man will not fight a woman; a good dog will not fight a chicken.

78．和尚口，吃遍四方；秀才口，骂遍四方。..........110
A monk's mouth eats everywhere; a scholar's mouth talks with curses for everything.

79．和尚念经，有口无心。..........111
A monk chants scripture with his mouth but not his heart.

80．猴子不钻圈，多筛几遍锣。..........112
If the monkey will not go through the hoop, he should tap the gong several times.

81．换汤不换药。..........113
Change the water but not the medicine.

82. 画蛇添足，多此一举。 114-115
Draw a snake, add a foot; one more unnecessary action.

83. 画虎不成反类犬。 116
Drew a tiger but it looks like a dog.

84. 皇帝不差饿兵。 117
Even a king cannot give orders to starving soldiers.

85. 皇帝不急，急死太监。 118
The emperor is not in a hurry but the eunuchs feel extremely hurried.

86. 皇帝的女儿不愁嫁。 119
An emperor's daughter need not worry about getting married.

87. 皇帝放个屁，州官唱台戏。 120
The emperor releases gas; state officials make an entire performance on the stage.

88. 黄鼠狼单咬病鸭子。 121
A weasel only bites a sick duck.

89. 黄鼠狼给鸡拜年——没安好心。 122
When a weasel says "Happy New Year" to the chicken, it's not with the best of intentions.

90. 会哭的孩子有奶吃。 123
The child who is good at crying gets the milk.

91. 浑水里好摸鱼。 124
It's easy to catch a fish in muddy water.

92. 活人不能叫尿憋死。 125
Living people can't kill themselves by refusing to urinate.

93. 饥不择食，寒不择衣，慌不择路，贫不择妻。 126
A hungry person is not picky about food; a cold person is not picky about clothes; a person who is nervous is not picky about an escape route; a poor person cannot be picky about a wife.

94. 鸡蛋里挑骨头。 127
Pick a bone from an egg.

95. 鸡窝里飞出个金凤凰。 128
A golden phoenix flies out from a chicken's nest.

96. 家花哪有野花香。 129
How can a home flower smell better then a wild flower?

97. 家家有本难念的经。 130
Every family has a difficult scripture to chant.

98. 嫁出去的女儿泼出去的水。 131
A daughter gets married off, just like water is poured out.

99. 嫁汉嫁汉，穿衣吃饭。 132
Marry a man for clothes and food.

100. 嫁鸡随鸡，嫁狗随狗，嫁了猴子满山走。........................133
If a woman marries a chicken, she has to follow the chicken; if she marries a dog, she must follow the dog; if she marries a monkey, she has to walk with the monkey all over the mountain.

101. 姜还是老的辣。..134
Nevertheless, the old ginger is hotter.

102. 姜太公钓鱼，愿者上钩。..................................135
Mr. Jiang is fishing; any fish who is willing can bite the hook.

103. 教会徒弟，饿死师傅。....................................136
The master teaches the apprentice to learn the task and the master starves to death.

104. 近水楼台先得月，向阳花木易为春。..........................137
The moon reflects first on the building with a terrace near the water; spring comes earlier to flowers and trees which face the sun.

105. 敬酒不吃吃罚酒。..138
Refuse a toast, then you will be forced to drink as punishment.

106. 敬了父母不怕天，纳了捐税不怕官。..........................139
If you show filial piety and respect for your parents, you have no need to be afraid of God's punishment; if you pay your taxes, no need to be afraid of the government officials.

107. 久病床前无孝子。..140
If a parent is sick too long, no dutiful children will be waiting in front of the bed.

108. 酒后吐真言。..141
After drinking some wine, you will tell the truth.

109. 酒是穿肠毒药，色是刮骨钢刀。..............................142
Wine is poison that passes through your gut; lust is like a knife that scrapes your bones.

110. 救急不救穷。..143
Help in emergencies; do not help the poor.

111. 口惠而实不至。..144
Promises are words, but not deeds.

112. 快刀切豆腐，两面光。....................................145
A sharp knife slices the bean curd; both sides are smooth.

113. 筷子头上出逆子，棒子底下出孝子。..........................146
With chopsticks, raise a disobedient son; with a stick, raise a dutiful son.

114. 癞蛤蟆想吃天鹅肉。......................................147
A toad wants to eat swan meat.

115. 懒驴子上磨屎尿多。......................................148
Once a lazy donkey starts working at the mill, he will have more excrement and urine then usual.

116. 懒婆娘的裹脚布，又臭又长。................................149
The cotton cloth binding a lazy woman's feet is too stinky and too long.

117. 老虎屁股摸不得。..150
Cannot touch a tiger's bottom.

118. 老虎头上拍苍蝇。..151
Swat a fly on a tiger's head.

119. 老鼠掉进米缸里。..152
A mouse drops in to a rice vat.

120. 老王卖瓜，自卖自夸。..153
Old Mr. Wang sells melons; he brags his melons are the best.

121. 老子偷瓜盗果，儿子杀人放火。..154
If a father steals melons and fruit, his son will kill people and set fires.

122. 礼下于人，必有所求。..155
If someone is overly polite, he must have a request.

123. 瓜田不纳履，李下不整冠。..156
Don't adjust your shoes when walking in a melon patch; don't rearrange your hat when walking under a palm tree.

124. 脸丑怪镜子。..157
Blame the mirror if your face is ugly.

125. 脸上带笑，袖里藏刀。..158
Smile on the face, but a knife hidden in the sleeve.

126. 龙居浅水遭虾戏，虎落平阳被犬欺。..159
If a dragon is living in the shallow water, it will be made a fool of by the shrimp; if a tiger meets with misfortune and comes to a plain and bright place, it will be humiliated by a dog.

127. 龙怕揭鳞，虎怕抽筋。..160
A dragon is afraid having its scales peeled off; a tiger is afraid of having its veins ripped out.

128. 龙生龙，凤生凤，老鼠生儿打地洞。..161
A dragon gives birth to a dragon; a phoenix gives birth to a phoenix; a mouse's son can only dig a hole in the ground.

129. 麻雀虽小，五脏俱全。..162
A sparrow though small still has all five internal organs.

130. 马行无力皆因瘦，人不风流只为贫。..163
A horse walks without strength because it is thin; a man has no women only because he has no money.

131. 买得起马，配不起鞍。..164
Can afford to buy a horse, cannot afford to buy a saddle.

132. 买衣服看袖子，讨老婆看舅子。..165
When buying clothes, pay attention to the sleeves; when taking a wife, look at the woman's brother.

133. 满口仁义道德，一肚子男盗女娼。..166
He always talks about virtue and morality, but always thinks about the dirty things as do ruffians and whores.

134. 猫哭老鼠假慈悲。..167
A cat crying for a mouse is a fake mercy.

135. 茅厕里的石头，又臭又硬。..168
A stone in the latrine, both stinky and hard.

136. 没吃过猪肉，还没见过猪跑？..169
If you have not eaten pig meat, have you seen pigs run yet?

137. 没了头的苍蝇，乱撞一气。..170
A fly without a head will be out of control and collide with anything it passes non-stop.

138. 没有家鬼，引不进外祟。..171
If the family does not have its own ghost, there will be no ghost to let outside evil spirits in.

139. 民怕兵匪抢，官怕纱帽丢，穷怕常生病，富怕贼人偷。...........172-173
People fear being robbed by soldiers or gangsters; officials fear losing their black gauz cap; poor people fear always being sick; rich people fear that a thief comes to steal.

140. 明修栈道，暗渡陈仓。..174
Construct a footway on the edge of a cliff in broad daylight; at the same time send troops in secret to the country town Chen Cang to attack the enemy.

141. 摸着石头过河。..175
Cross the river by feeling the stones.

142. 母狗不掉尾，公狗不上身。..176
If a bitch does not waggle her tail, a male dog cannot mount her.

143. 母以子为贵，妻以夫为荣。..177
A mother can be more valuable because of her son; a wife can be proud of marrying a powerful husband.

144. 牡丹花下死，做鬼也风流。..178
To die under a Mu Dan flower, even becoming a ghost, is still romantic.

145. 木偶能跳动，自有提线人。..179
A wooden puppet can jump and move around; of course there is the person who pulls the strings.

146. 哪有猫儿不偷惺。..180
How can a cat not steal raw meat or fish?

147. 男怕入错行，女怕嫁错郎。..181
A man is afraid of choosing the wrong occupation; a woman is afraid of marrying the wrong man.

148. 你走你的阳关道，我走我的独木桥。..182
You walk on your Yangguan Avenue; I walk on my single plank bridge.

149. 宁逢恶宾，勿逢故人。..183
Rather run into an evil visitor than an old friend or acquaintance.

150. 宁借人停丧，不借人成双。..184-185
Rather lend people a room to park a coffin than lend a couple the room for a wedding.

151. 宁为鸡首，勿为牛后。..186
Rather be a chicken's head than a cow's butt.

152. 宁愿独偷一只鸡，不愿合偷一头牛。..187
Rather steal a chicken by yourself than steal a cow with others.

153. 牛头伸到马槽里。..188
A cow's head stretched out into a horse's manger.

154. 女人偷人隔层纸，男人偷人隔座山。...........................189
When a woman commits adultery, between the man and woman there is only a piece of paper; when a man commits adultery, there is a mountain between the man and the woman.

155. 跑得了和尚跑不了庙。...190
The monk can run away but not the temple.

156. 蚍蜉撼大树，可笑不自量。.....................................191
The big ant tries to shake the big tree; very funny because it overestimates its own strength.

157. 七十不留宿，八十不留餐 。....................................192
Do not urge a seventy year old to stay overnight; do not urge an eighty year old to eat in your home.

158. 妻不如妾，妾不如偷，偷得着还不如偷不着 。....................193
A wife is not as good as a concubine; a concubine is not as good as having an affair; having had an affair is not as good as the anticipation of having an affair.

159. 千里之堤，溃于一蚁之穴。.....................................194
A 500 kilometer dam breaks because of one ant's nest.

160. 前人栽树，后人乘凉。...195
The earlier generation plants the tree; the later generations relax in the cool shade of the tree.

161. 枪打出头鸟。...196
The gun always shoots the bird with its head stuck out.

162. 强龙斗不过地头蛇。...197
A powerful dragon can't win against a snake in its own territory.

163. 强扭的瓜不甜。...198
Pick a melon by twisting the stem with force and the melon will not be sweet.

164. 巧媚眼做给瞎子看。...199
Make a cute, sexy glance at a blind person.

165. 窃钩者诛，窃国者侯。...200
A petty thief who steals the hook of a clothing bag is executed; a big thief who steals the country will have a noble title conferred upon him.

166. 情人眼里出西施。...201
From a lover's eye even an ordinary woman comes out as beautiful as Xi Shi.

167. 请神容易送神难。...202
Inviting a god to come in is easy; getting rid of him is difficult.

168. 穷算命，富烧香。...203
Poor people see the fortune teller; rich people burn joss sticks.

169. 人多懒，龙多旱，鸡多不下蛋。.................................204
The more people there are, the lazier they get; the more dragons there are, the drier the weather; the more chickens the fewer the eggs.

170．人急悬梁，狗急跳墙。..205
Put people under heavy pressure, and they will hang themselves from the roof beam; put pressure on a dog, and it will jump over the wall.

171．人怕出名猪怕壮。..206
People are afraid to be well known just like a pig is afraid to be stout and strong.

172．人穷志短，马瘦毛长。..207
If a person is poor, his ambition is low. If a horse is skinny, his hair looks longer.

173．人虽有千算，天只有一算，天若容人算，世上无穷汉。..........208-209
Even if people calculate a thousand times, God only decides once; if God allowed people to decide their lives, there would be no poor Chinese man in this world.

174．人无横财不富，马无野草不肥。................................210
If people don't have a windfall, they cannot be rich; if a horse doesn't eat wild grass, the horse cannot be fat.

175．人要倒霉，喝口凉水也塞牙。..................................211
If a person has bad luck, even if he drinks cold water the water will stick in his teeth.

176．人一走，茶就凉。..212
The person just left; his tea has gotten cold.

177．肉包子打狗，有去无回。......................................213
Hit a dog with a meat-stuffed bun, and the bun will not be coming back.

'178．如鱼饮水，冷暖自知。......................................214
As the fish drinks the water, the fish knows if the water's temperature is cold or warm.

179．入国问禁，入境问俗。..215
Ask for the taboos when you enter an another country, ask for the local customs when you enter a new place.

180．入门休问荣枯事，观看容颜便得知。............................216
When you enter the house, don't ask people if business is good or bad; just look at the host's face and you know what is going on.

181．塞翁失马，焉知非福。..217
The old man from the frontier fortress lost his horse; how do you know this is not a good fortune?

182．三天不打，上房揭瓦。....................................218-219
If you don't beat the children for three days, they will climb on the house and peel off the roof tiles.

183．三代富贵始知饮食。..220
After three generations you have wealth and social position; then you start to know how to drink and eat.

184．三岁看大，七岁看老。..221
Look at a three year old boy, and you can tell what he will look like when he grows up; look at a seven year old boy, and you can tell what he will look like when he is very old.

185．山中无老虎，猴子称大王。................................222-223
When the tiger is off the mountain, the monkey is king.

186．山高皇帝远。..224
The mountains are high and the emperor is far away.

187．善泳者溺，善骑者堕。..225
People good at swimming will drown; people good at horseback riding will fall.

188．上贼船容易，下贼船难。..226
Getting on a pirate's boat is easy; getting off is hard.

189．烧香的赶出和尚。..227
People who come to the temple burn joss sticks and drive the monks away.

190．少年夫妻老来伴。..228
When a husband and wife are young, life is all passion; when they get older, it is companionship.

191．生米煮成了熟饭。..229
When rice has been cooked, it's too late to change it back to uncooked rice.

192．生男是弄璋之喜，生女是弄瓦之喜。..230
Having a boy is like the joy of playing with jade; having a girl is like the joy of playing with a roof tile.

193．盛喜中不许人物，盛怒中不答人简。..231
If you are in an extremely happy mood, don't promise people gifts; if you are in an extremely angry mood, don't reply to people's letters.

194．诗为酒友，酒是色媒。..232
Poems make drunkards friends; wine is the aphrodisiac for sex.

195．十年修得同船渡，百年修得共枕眠。..233
Pray for ten years and in their next life two persons can cross the river in the same boat; pray one hundred years and in their next life two persons can be married and share a pillow to sleep.

196．拾得鸡毛当令箭。..234
Pick up a chicken feather and treat it as an army commander's arrow.

197．士可杀，不可辱。..235
You can kill intellectuals but you cannot insult them.

198．世上无不散的筵席。..236-237
In this world if there is no feast, people will not leave.

199．事后诸葛亮。..238
Zhu Ge Liang's wisdom came after things happened.

200．柿子拣软的捏。..239
Choose the soft persimmon to squeeze.

201．授人以鱼，不如授人以渔。..240
Rather teach the person how to fish than just give him the fish.

202．瘦死的骆驼比马大。..241
The camel died because it was too skinny but it was still bigger than a horse.

203. 书中自有黄金屋，书中自有千钟粟，书中自有颜如玉。..........242-243
There is a golden house in books; there is a high salary in books; there is a beautiful woman in books.

204. 树倒猢狲散。..244
When the tree falls, the monkeys on the tree scatter.

205. 树高千丈，叶落归根。....................................245
No matter how tall the tree, its leaves will fall around its roots.

206. 水浅养不住大鱼。..246
A big fish cannot grow up in shallow water.

207. 水至清则无鱼，人至察则无徒。............................247
If the water is too clean, there are no fish; nobody will deal with people who nitpick on details.

208. 顺我者昌，逆我者亡。....................................248
The people who obey me will be prosperous; the people who disobey will be executed.

209. 说话听声，锣鼓听音。....................................249
Listen to people talk, listen to their voices; listen to the gongs and drums, listen to their tempo.

210. 送佛送到西天。......................................250-251
If you send Buddha to West Heaven, you must accompany him until he arrives.

211. 死了张屠夫，不吃浑毛猪。................................252
Zhang the butcher is dead; we still don't eat the pig with hair.

212. 死马当作活马医。..253
Medical treatment for a dead horse as if it were a live horse.

213. 死猪不怕开水烫。..254
A dead pig is not afraid of being scalded by boiling water.

214. 螳臂挡车，不自量力。....................................255
A mantis tried to stop a cart; he overestimated his physical strength.

215. 孙猴子跳不出如来佛的掌心。..........................256-257
The Monkey Sun cannot jump out of Ru Lain Buddha's palm.

216. 螳螂捕蝉，黄雀在后。....................................258
A mantis is catching a cicada but a finch is hunting right behind the mantis.

217. 天冷冷在风，人穷穷在债。................................259
When the winter wind blows, it is even colder; when people are in debt they are even poorer.

218. 太太死了压断街，老爷死了没人抬。....................260-261
When the wife died, her funeral procession blocked the street's traffic; when her husband died, nobody carried the coffin.

219. 天上掉馅饼。..262
A meat pie drops from the sky.

220. 铜盆碰到铁扫帚，恶人自有恶人磨。........................263
A copper pot hits an iron broom; evil people naturally will have evil people to torture them.

221. 偷鸡不着蚀把米。..264
Failed to steal the chicken, instead lost the rice in his hand.

222．兔子不吃窝边草。..265
The rabbit does not eat the grass by the side of the nest.

223．脱裤子放屁，多此一举。......................................266
Taking off your pants to release gas is one more unnecessary action.

224．歪嘴和尚念真经。..267
A monk's twisted mouth chants the real scriptures.

225．万恶淫为首，百善孝为先。....................................268
Among all the evil things, promiscuity is the first; among all the virtues, filial obedience is the first.

226．王子犯法，与庶民同罪。......................................269
If a prince breaks the law, he will be punished as a common person.

227．为人不做亏心事，半夜敲门心不惊。............................270
A person who does not do unfair things to others will not be frightened when somebody knocks on the door at midnight.

228．文武之道，一张一弛。..271
The logic of managing the country by King Zhou Wenwang and King Zhou Wuwang is that sometimes a tight policy is used, sometimes a lenient policy.

229．卧榻之侧，岂容他人酣睡。....................................272
How could you allow other people to sleep soundly on your side of the bed ?

230．无敌国外患者，国恒亡。......................................273
If a country is surrounded with no enemies and trouble from outside, the country will die out.

231．无事不登三宝殿。..274-275
People never go to the San Bao temple except if they want something.

232．无官一身轻， 有子万事足。...................................276
If you are not an official, you can totally relax; if you have a son, you will be totally satisfied.

233．无冤不成夫妻，无债不成父子。................................277
If no injustice from the last life, no need to be a married couple in this life; if no debt from last life, no need to be father and son in this life.

234．物必先腐而后虫生之，人必自侮而后人侮之。...............278-279
Things must spoil first, then the worm will grow; a person must insult himself first, then other people will insult him.

235．喜时之言多失信，怒时之言多失体。............................280
When people talk in a happy mood, many times they lose credit; when people talk in a angry mood, many times they lose dignity.

236．瞎猫撞上死耗子。..281
A blind cat collides with a dead mouse.

237．夏虫不可与语冰。..282
You cannot discuss ice with a summer worm.

238．先小人，后君子。..283
First act as a villain, then act as a gentleman.

239．鲜花插在牛粪上。..284
A fresh flower stuck in cow manure.

240．闲时不烧香，急时抱佛脚。..................................285
People don't burn joss sticks when they have leisure time; they hold Buddha's feet in their arms during emergencies.

241．项庄舞剑，意在沛公。..................................286-287
Xiang Zhuang dances with a double-edged straight sword; his objective is Pei Gong.

242．响鼓不用重锤敲。......................................288
You don't have to use a heavy hammer to beat on a loud drum.

243．小不忍则乱大谋。......................................289
If you do not put up with little things, you will jeopardize a big strategy.

244．小儿欲得安，常带三分饥和寒。............................290
If you want the little baby to be safe and well, keep it 30% hungry and cold.

245．小脚一双，眼泪一缸。..................................291
One pair of small feet costs one bucket of tears.

246．笑贫不笑娼。..292
People ridicule the poor but not whores.

247．新官上任三把火。......................................293
A new official sets a fire three times on the first day of his job.

248．秀才遇到兵，有理说不清。..............................294-295
A scholar runs into a soldier; even with right on his side, the scholar cannot reason with him.

249．油盐爆炒不进的鹅卵石。................................296
Cobblestones cannot absorb the flavor of oil and salt by stir-frying.

250．有朋自远方来，不亦乐乎。..............................297
How happy we are to meet a friend who has come from a far away place.

251．徐娘半老，风韵犹存。..................................298
Madam Xu in her middle age was still very sexy.

252．血缘亲，打断骨头连着筋。..............................299
Blood relationship is intimate; bones may snap into two but veins still link together.

253．衙门朝南开，有理没钱莫进来。........................300-301
The court opens to the south; if you are in the right but don't have money, don't enter.

254．要想一天不舒服，穿双小鞋子；要想一辈子不舒服，有两个女人。.302-303
If you want to be unhappy for a day, wear a pair of shoes that are too small; if you want to be unhappy for life, have two women.

255．阎王好见小鬼难当。....................................304
It's easy to deal with the king of hell, but not with a little ghost.

256．羊肉没吃到，惹了一身羊膻臭。..........................305
Didn't eat the mutton but still stinks like sheep.

257. 一个和尚挑水喝，两个和尚抬水喝，三个和尚没水喝。...........306-307
One monk with a pole on his shoulder carries two buckets of water to drink; two monks with a pole on their shoulders carry a bucket of water to drink; three monks have no water to drink.

258. 养儿防老，积谷防饥。....................................308
Raise children to provide for old age, just like saving the unhusked rice to provide against hunger.

259. 野草难肥胎瘦马，横财不富命穷人。..........................309
Wild grass cannot make a skinny horse fat if it was thin in the womb; money that comes suddenly cannot make a person rich whom fate has made poor.

260. 一篙子打沉一船人。....................................310
One stroke with the bamboo pole against the boat and all the people on the boat sink.

261. 一粒老鼠屎，坏了一锅汤。................................311
One small piece of mouse shit can spoil a whole pot of soup.

262. 一人得道，鸡犬升天。....................................312
A person rises in power and becomes important; even his chickens and dogs will rise to the sky.

263. 一碗米养个恩人，一斗米养个仇人。..........................313
Give a person one bowl of rice and you are a benefactor; give a person much more rice, then you will create an enemy.

264. 一朝被蛇咬，十年怕井绳。................................314
Once bitten by a snake, afraid of a well rope for ten years.

265. 一人造反，株连九族。....................................315
One person rebels against the government and punishment will be visited on nine families who are relations.

266. 一山容不下二虎。......................................316
One mountain cannot hold two tigers.

267. 一桶水不响，半桶水晃荡。................................317
A full bucket of water makes no noise; a bucket half full of water shakes.

268. 宜未雨而稠缪，勿临渴而掘井。.............................318
Tie up the doors and windows before it rains; do not wait to dig a well until you are thirsty.

269. 以小人之心，度君子之腹。................................319
Small people use their little minds to guess what gentlemen think.

270. 饮水不忘掘井人。......................................320
When you drink water, don't forget about the people who dug the well.

271. 英雄难过美人关。......................................321
Even heroes can't resist the temptation of beauty.

272. 硬汉难避枕边风。.................................322-323
Even a tough man has a hard time not listening to a woman's pillow talk.

273. 油盐爆炒不进的鹅卵石。..................................324
Cobblestones cannot absorb the flavor of oil and salt by stir-frying.

274. 有朋自远方来，不亦乐乎。..............................325
How happy we are to meet a friend who has come from a far away place.

275. 有钱能使鬼推磨。..............................326
Money can make a ghost push a millwheel.

276. 有枪就是草头王。..............................327
The man with the gun is the local king.

277. 有眼不识泰山。..............................328
A person has eyes but cannot recognize Tai Shan mountain.

278. 又要马儿跑得快，又要马儿不吃草。..............................329
One expectation is that the horse runs fast; another is that there is no need to feed the horse.

279. 又要做婊子，又要立牌坊。..............................330
One woman expects to be a whore, but the other expects to be rewarded with a monumental archway.

280. 鱼见食而不见钩，人见利而不见害。..............................331
Fish see the worm but not the hook; people see the benefits but not the harm.

281. 鱼找鱼，虾找虾，王八找的鳖亲家。..............................332
Fish look for fish; shrimp look for shrimp; turtles look for soft-shelled turtles to be their relatives through their children's marriage.

282. 欲加之罪，何患无词。..............................333
If I want to make a person guilty, why should I worry about a reason.

283. 鹬蚌相持，渔人得利。..............................334
When the snipe and the clam grapple, the fisherman profits.

284. 远来的和尚会念经。..............................335
The monk who comes from far away is better at reciting the scriptures.

285. 债多不愁，虱多不痒。..............................336
Have too many debts and you don't worry; have too many lice and you don't feel an itch.

286. 占着茅坑不拉屎。..............................337
Take over a latrine but not to shit.

287. 站着借，跪着讨。..............................338
You can stand to lend money out; you must kneel to ask for money back.

288. 针插不进，水泼不进。..............................339
A needle can't stick in and splashed water can't enter.

289. 知己知彼，百战不殆。..............................340
Know yourself and know your enemy; fight hundreds of battles with no danger of defeat.

290. 只见贼吃肉，没见贼挨打。..............................341
Only see the thief eat the meat; not see the thief suffer from a beating.

291. 只许州官放火，不许百姓点灯。..............................342
Only state officials are allowed to set a fire; common people are not allowed to light a lamp.

292. 忠臣不侍二君，烈女不嫁二夫。..............................343
A loyal official cannot serve two emperors; a chaste widow is ready to follow her husband in death and not remarry.

293. 重赏之下必有勇夫，香饵之下必有死鱼。 344-345
For a handsome reward, you will be sure to attract a brave man; with sweet-smelling bait, you will be sure to find a dead fish.

294. 种瓜得瓜，种豆得豆。 346
Plant melons, harvest melons; plant beans, harvest beans.

295. 竹篮打水一场空。 347
Use a bamboo basket to scoop up water and it comes up empty.

296. 煮熟的鸭子又飞了。 348
A cooked duck flies out again.

297. 捉贼捉赃，捉奸捉双。 349
If you catch a thief, you must recover the stolen goods; if you catch adulterers, you must catch them both.

298. 自古红颜多薄命。 350
From ancient times the majority of beautiful women have had short lives.

299. 坐如钟，站如松，卧如弓，行如风。 351
Sit like a clock, stand like a pine tree, sleep like a bow, walk like the wind.

300. 做弱者不得好活，做强者不得好死。 352
A loser cannot have a comfortable life; a dictator cannot have a good way to die.

ài zhī yù qí shēng è zhī yù qí sǐ
爱 之 欲 其 生，恶 之 欲 其 死。

Proverb: Love somebody, wish him a long life; hate somebody, wish he would die.

Comment: A person simly follow his own love and hate, without principle.

ài
爱：love

zhī
之：it, here means he or she

yù
欲：want or wish

qí
其：it, here means the person

shēng
生：alive; here means have a long life

ài zhī yù qí shēng
爱 之 欲 其 生：love somebody, wish he or she has a long life

è
恶：hate

è zhī
恶 之：hate him or her

sǐ
死：die

è zhī yù qí sǐ
恶 之 欲 其 死：hate somebody, wish he or she would die

喜爱一个人时就想让他长寿，讨厌一个人时就想把他除掉。指对待人物或处理事情单纯从个人的爱憎好恶出发，没有什么原则性。

bǎi zú zhī chóng sǐ ér bù jiāng
百 足 之 虫， 死 而 不 僵。

Proverb: A hundred foot long bug is dead but it's still not stiff.
Comment: Some big family or group is no longer in power but they still have strong influence.

bǎi
百：hundred

zú
足：foot

zhī
之：'s

chóng
虫：worm, bug

mǎi zú zhī chóng
百 足 之 虫：a hundred foot bug

sī
死：die, death

ér
而：but

bù
不：not

jiāng jiāng yìng
僵 = 僵 硬：stiff

sǐ ér bù jiāng
死 而 不 僵：died, but it's still not stiff

百足：一种多足的爬虫，躯干多节，死了身子也不僵化。比喻有权势的家族或集团，即使衰败了，也会残留着相当的势力和影响。

bāo zi yǒu nòu bú zài zhě shàng
包 子 有 肉 不 在 褶 上。

Proverb: You can not tell how much meat the steamed buns have inside from the fold of the buns.

Comment: You can't tell people's ability, talent, identity and wealth just by the way they look.

bāo zi
包 子：steamed buns

yǒu
有：have

ròu
肉：meat

bāo zi yǒu ròu
包 子 有 肉：the steamed buns with meat stuffing

zài
在：exist

bú zài
不 在：not exist, be absent

zhě
褶：fold

shàng
上：above, on top of

zhě shàng
褶 上：on the fold of the buns

bú zài zhě shàng
不 在 褶 上：you can not tell how much meat the steamed buns have inside from the fold of the buns

褶子：包子上面的褶皱。比喻人的才能、身份、财富光从外表是看不出来的。

bǎo ān shì shì yōng kāi yǎn huì jìn rén qíng zhǐ diǎn tóu

饱谙世事慵开眼，会尽人情只点头。

Proverb: When something happens, a person who has a full understanding of the ways of the world will not bother to open his eyes; he only bows his head, appearing to agree.

Comment: If a person sees through a trick or conspiracy, he will not tell what he is really thinking, and he will just echo what others say.

bǎo
饱：be full with hunger satisfied

ān
谙：fully understand

shì　shì jiè shàng
世 = 世界上：all of the world

shì
事：thing, affair

bǎo ān shì shì
饱谙世事：fully understands world affairs

yōng　yōng lān
慵 = 慵懒：lethargic

kāi
开：open

yān
眼：eyes

huì　lǐng huì
会 = 领会：understand

jìn
尽：within the limits of

rén qíng
人情：the ways of the world

zhǐ
只：only

diǎn tóu
点头：bows his head, here means appearing to agree

huì jìn rén qíng zhǐ diǎn tóu
会尽人情只点头：fully understand the ways of the world, only bows his head

通晓人情世故的人遇事懒得睁开眼，尽可能装聋作哑多点头。指把人情看得很透的人，遇事轻易不表态，采取附和的态度。

bèi tā yī dǐng jiào qǐ tā yī gè hào kè tā yī bù gǎo qū tā yī gè xiǎo
备它一顶轿, 起它一个号, 刻它一部稿, 娶它一个小。

Proverb: (1) Prepare a sedan chair, (2) adopt an elegant pseudonym, (3) carve an article on wood, and (4) get a young concubine.

Comment: Once intellectuals succeeded in the Ming and Ching Dynasty examinations, they thought they were different from others. They did these four things first. (1) Wealthy people had a sedan chair for traveling, (2) intellectuals chose a special name for social reasons, (3) the wood was used to print articles to be famous, and (4) rich men had concubines.

bèi zhūn bèi
备 = 准 备：prepare

tā
它：it; here means things

yī
一：one

dǐng
顶：a measure word for sedan chair

yī dǐng jiào
一顶 轿：one sedan chair

qǐ tā
起 它：give it

gè
个：a measure word for name

yī gè hào
一个 号：an elegant pseudonym

kè tā
刻 它：carve it

bù
部：a measure word for article

yī bù gǎo
一 部 稿：an article

qū
娶：marry

qū tā
娶 它：marry it

gè
个：a measure word for people

xiǎo
小：little

yī gè xiǎo
一个 小：a concubine

旧时读书人一旦中举，就觉得自己与众不同，首先要做四件事：备他一顶轿子——当时有钱人的交通工具。给自己起一个对外交际时用的雅号，刻他一部自己写的稿子好进行个人宣传。像有钱人一样讨一房年轻漂亮的小老婆。

bèi wō lǐ fàng pì zāo tā zì jǐ
被 窝 里 放 屁，糟 蹋 自 己。

Proverb: Spoil yourself by releasing gas under the blanket.
Comment: This is a sarcastic expression because a person is forced to smell his own gas. This saying describes people who stupidly work against themselves.

bèi bèi zī
被 = 被 子：blanket

wō
窝：a nest

lǐ lǐ miàn
里 = 里 面：inside

bèi wō lǐ
被 窝 里：under the blanket

fàng pì
放 屁：release gas

zāo tā
糟 蹋：spoil

zì jǐ
自 己：oneself

zāo tā zì jǐ
糟 蹋 自 己：spoil oneself

bèi wō lǐ fàng pì zāo tā zì jǐ
被 窝 里 放 屁 糟 蹋 自 己：spoil oneself by releasing gas under the blanket

屁是臭的，强迫自己闻臭屁。比喻有些人做的事情正好和自己过不去。

biàn xì fǎ dē mán bú guò dǎ luó dē
变 戏 法 的 瞒 不 过 打 锣 的。

Proverb: The person who performs the magic tricks cannot hide the secret from the person who beats the gong.

Comment: In a traditional Chinese magic show, before the magician comes out, someone beats the gong for atmosphere. You cannot keep secrets from people who know the inside information and the real story.

biàn
变：change

xì fǎ
戏 法：magic tricks

biàn xì fǎ
变 戏 法：perform the magic tricks

dē
的：'s

biàn xì fǎ dē
变 戏 法 的：the person who performs the magic tricks

mán
瞒：conceal, hide

mán bú guò
瞒 不 过：can not hide the secret

dǎ
打：beat

luó
锣：gong

dǎ luó dē
打 锣 的：the person who beat the gong

mán bú guò dǎ luó dē
瞒 不 过 打 锣 的：can not hide the secret from the person who beat the gong

中国人变戏法之前以打锣帮场，指打锣的最了解变戏法的内幕。
比喻捣鬼瞒不过了解底细的人。

bìng jí luàn tóu yī
病 急 乱 投 医。

Proverb: When very sick and in urgent need of help, see any doctor, no matter good or bad.
Comment: When you have a serious problem, seek assistance wherever you can get it.

bìng
病：an illness, sick

jí
急：urgent

luàn
乱：in disorder, without thinking or planning

tóu
投：throw oneself into

yī yī shēng
医 = 医 生：doctor

tóu yī
投 医：see a doctor as a patient

luàn tóu yī
乱 投 医：see any doctor

bìng jí luàn tóu yī
病 急 乱 投 医：when very sick and in urgent need of help, see any doctor no matter good or bad

病势危重时慌乱地到处请医生。比喻事情紧急，顾不上选择对象和办法，盲目求人。

The swastika is an ancient Buddhist symbol associated with good fortune and happiness, and it is frequently found on Buddhist statuary. The Nazis expropriated and reversed this symbol. In Asia, the traditional swastika has no connection with Hitler or Nazism and precedes both by thousands of years.

bú dào xī tiān bù zhī fó dà xiǎo
不 到 西 天 不 知 佛 大 小。

Proverb: If you don't reach the western paradise, you will not know how big the Buddha is.

Comment: The western paradise is the place where the Buddha lives. This proverb is said as an apology to some important person for not recognizing who they are.

bú
不：no, not

dào
到：reach, arrive

xī tiān
西 天：western paradise, the place where the Buddha lives

zhī zhī dào
知 = 知 道：know

bù zhī
不 知：not know

fó
佛：Buddha

dà
大：big

xiǎo
小：small

dà xiǎo
大 小：size; here means here means the Buddha's size

bú dào xī tiān bù zhī fó dà xiǎo
不 到 西 天 不 知 佛 大 小：if you don't reach the western paradise, you will not know how big the Buddha is

西天：佛所居住的西方极乐世界。不经过亲身实践，就不能得到深刻认识和感受，也比喻不到时候，不知某人地位高低。

bǔ dé lǎo shǔ dǎ pò yóu píng
捕 得 老 鼠，打 破 油 瓶。

Proverb: One way to catch a mouse is to hit the cooking oil bottle; the mouse is caught, but the bottle is broken into bits.

Comment: The mouse is attracted to the cooking oil. The loss of the oil outweighs the gain from getting rid of the mouse.

bǔ
捕：catch

dé
得：no meaning, used after a verb to indicate can or certainly

lǎo shǔ
老 鼠：a mouse

bǔ dé lǎo shǔ
捕 得 老 鼠：caught a mouse

dǎ
打：hit

pò
破：break

yóu píng
油 瓶：a oil bottle; here means a cooking oil bottle

dǎ pò yóu píng
打 破 油 瓶：break the cooking oil bottle into bits

因为只想着要捕捉老鼠，反而失手打破了油瓶。比喻做事考虑不周全，得不偿失。

bù guǎn hēi māo bái māo néng zhuā lǎo shǔ jiù shì hǎo māo
不 管 黑 猫 白 猫，能 抓 老 鼠 就 是 好 猫。

Proverb: No matter if the cat is black or white, if it can catch a mouse, it is a good cat.

Comment: Deng Xiaoping said this when he introduced capitalist-style reforms into the Chinese economy.

bù guǎn
不 管：no matter

hēi
黑：black

bái
白：white

māo
猫：cat

hēi mō
黑 猫：black cat

bái mō
白 猫：white cat.

néng
能：can

zhuā
抓：catch

lǎo shǔ
老 鼠：mouse

jiù shì
就 是：at this point

hǎo
好：good

hǎo māo
好 猫：a good cat

néng zhuā lǎo shǔ jiù shì hǎo māo
能 抓 老 鼠 就 是 好 猫：if it can catch a mouse it is a good cat

不管什么颜色的猫，只要能抓老鼠就是好猫。比喻不论是什么人，或不论用什么方法，只要能达到预期的目的就行.

bú jiàn guān cái bú diào lèi
不见 棺材 不 掉 泪。

Proverb: If you do not see the coffin, you won't cry.

Comment: Some people only give up when something has totally failed and cannot be retrieved. Only then will they regret what has happened.

bú
不：no, not.

jiàn làn jiàn
见 = 看 见：see

bú jiàn
不 见：not see

guān cái
棺 材：a coffin; here means a totally bad situation

diào
掉：fall, drop

lèi
泪：tears

diào lèi
掉 泪：cry, here means regret

bú jiàn guān cái bú diào lèi
不 见 棺 材不 掉 泪：If you do not see the coffin, you won't cry

比喻人不到彻底失败的时候不肯罢休。指只有在事情坏到不可挽回时，才会有悔恨之意。

bú	jiàn	tù	zi	bù	sā	yīng
不	见	兔	子	不	撒	鹰。

Proverb: Until you see the rabbit, don't release the falcon.

Comment: Do not take action until you are sure.

bú
不：no, not

jiàn　kàn jiàn
见 = 看 见：see

bú jiàn
不 见：not see

tù zi
兔 子：a rabbit

yīng
鹰：a falcon

sā
撒：release

bù sā
不 撒：not release

bù sā yīng
不撒 鹰：don't release the falcon

bú jiàn tù zi bù sā yīng
不 见 兔 子 不撒 鹰：until you see the rabbit, don't release the falcon

还没有看见兔子的时候，就不要早早地把猎鹰放出去，不但白费力气还要坏了事。比喻没有把握达到预期的目的，就不采取行动。

bù kàn sēng miàn kàn fó miàn bú niàn yú qíng niàn shuǐ qíng
不看僧面看佛面，不念鱼情念水情。

Proverb: If you don't give a monk face, you should give Buddha face; if you don't give a fish face, you should give the water face.
Comment: Giving someone "face" is very important in Chinese culture. In this, if you don't respect the person, you still should respect the people behind him or her who have more power and influence.

bú
不：no, not

kàn
看：look at

miàn miàn zī
面 = 面子：face

kàn miàn zī
看面子：give face

sēng
僧：a monk

fó
佛：Buddha

kàn sēng miàn
看僧面：give monk face

kàn fó miàn
看佛面：give Buddha face

bú kàn sēng miàn kàn fó miàn
不看僧面看佛面：if not give monk face, should give Buddha face

niàn
念：consider

qíng gǎn qíng
情 = 感情：feelings

yú
鱼：fish

niàn yú qíng
念鱼情：consider a fish's feelings, give the fish face

shuǐ
水：water

niàn shuǐ qíng
念水情：consider water's feelings, give the water face

bú niàn yú qíng niàn shuǐ qíng
不念鱼情念水情：If you don't give the fish face, you should give the water face

鱼情、水情：这种面子或那种面子。比喻处理一件事，不看当事人的面子，也要看他的长辈或顾及他后面的比他地位更高和更有权势的人的情面。

bù néng liú fāng bǎi shì yě yào yí chòu wàn nián
不能留芳百世，也要遗臭万年。

Proverb: If you can't leave a good name in history, then leave a bad name.
Comment: To be famous is the most important thing. It doesn't matter how you accomplish it.

bù
不：no, not

néng
能：can

liú
留：leave

fāng fāng xiāng
芳 = 芳香：sweet smell

liú fāng
留芳：leave a well-known name

bǎi
百：hundred

shì shì dài
世 = 世代：generations

bǎi shì
百世：in history

bù néng liú fāng bǎi shì
不能留芳百世：if I cannot leave a good name in history

yě
也：also

yào
要：want

yí yí liú
遗 = 遗留：leave

chòu
臭：a bad smell

wàn
万：ten thousand

nián
年：year

wàn nián
万年：a long time, in history

yě yào yí chòu wàn nián
也要遗臭万年：then leave a bad name in history

不管当好人还是当坏人，只要能出名就行。

bú pà zéi tōu jiù pà zéi diàn jì
不怕贼偷，就怕贼惦记。

Proverb: Don't be afraid of being robbed by a thief; just be afraid the thief will think about you all the time.
Comment: This is said to warn people to be alert that some people might secretly be against you.

bú
不：no, not

pà
怕：afraid

zéi
贼：thief

tōu
偷：steal, rob

bú pà zéi tōu
不 怕 贼 偷：not afraid of being robbed

jiù
就：just

jiù pà
就 怕：just afraid

diàn jì
惦 记：be concerned, think about someone or something all the time

jiù pà zéi diàn jì
就 怕 贼 惦 记：just be afraid the thief will think about you all the time

惦记：一直想着。指贼要是盯上你的财物，迟早会下手。也指要警惕有人暗中算计。

bù qiú yǒu gōng dàn qiú wú guò
不求有功，但求无过。

Proverb: Don't demand for credit; only wish that you didn't make a mistake.
Comment: This is an ultra-cautious strategy that precludes originality and risk taking. It reflects traditional conservative Chinese culture.

bù
不：no, not.

qiú
求：demand, request

yǒu
有：have

gōng gōng láo
功 = 功劳：credit

bù qiú yǒu gōng
不求有功：don't demand for credit

dàn
但：only

wú méi yǒu
无 = 没有：without

guò guò shī
过 = 过失：a fault, a mistake

dàn qiú wú guò
但求无过：only wish that you didn't make a mistake

不想有多大的成就和功绩，只要不出错就行了。指一种安于现状不求进取的心态。

bú rù hǔ xuè yān dé hǔ zǐ
不 入 虎 穴，焉 得 虎 子？

Proverb: If you do not enter the tiger's den, how can you catch the baby tiger?
Comment: If you do not take risks, you can't obtain success.

bú
不：no, not

rù
入：enter

hǔ
虎：tiger

xuè
穴：den

bú rù hǔ xuè
不入虎穴：If you do not enter the tiger's den

yān
焉：how

dé
得：get, catch

zǐ
子：son

hǔ zǐ
虎子：baby tiger

yān dé hǔ zǐ
焉得虎子：how can you catch the baby tiger

焉：怎么，如何。不进老虎洞，怎么能捉到小老虎？比喻不冒风险，就不能获得成功。

bú xiào yǒu sān wú hòu wéi dà
不 孝 有 三，无 后 为 大。

Proverb: There are three things that show a man is devoted to his parents; among these, having a son is the most important.
Comment: In traditional China the three things a son should do were (1) take care of his parents, (2) have harmony among brothers, and (3) have a son. A family without a son can't continue, and this served as an excuse to let a husband bring a concubine into the home.

bú
不：no, not

xiào
孝：show devote for parents as moral goodness

yǒu
有：have

sān
三：three

yǒu sān
有 三：have three things

bú xiào yǒu sān
不 孝 有 三：there are three things that show a man is devoted to his parents

wú
无：not have

hòu hòu dài
后 = 后 代：later generations, here means a son

wéi
为：become

dà
大：big

wéi dà
为 大：is the most important

wú hòu wéi dà
无 后 为 大：having a son is the most important

无后：没有后代。不孝有三：第一不供养父母，第二兄弟不睦，第三没有子嗣。旧时认为这三种不孝中，没有子嗣是最严重的。

bù zuò zéi xīn bù jīng bù chī yú zuǐ bù xīng
不做贼，心不惊；不吃鱼，嘴不腥。

Proverb: If you are not a thief, you will not be frightened; if you do not eat the fish, you will have no stinking smell in the mouth.
Comment: If you didn't do a bad thing, you don't have to be afraid of being found out.

bú
不：no, not

zuò
做：do, be

zéi
贼：a thief

bú zuò zéi
不做贼：not a thief

xīn
心：heart

jīng jīng xià
惊 = 惊吓：frightened

bú zuò zéi xīn bù jīng
不做贼，心不惊：if you not a thief, will not be frightened

chī
吃：eat

yú
鱼：fish

zuǐ
嘴：mouth

xīng xīng chòu
腥 = 腥臭：stinking smell

bù chī yú zuǐ bù xīng
不吃鱼，嘴不腥：if not eat the fish, no stinking smell in the mouth

不做坏事就用不着担惊受怕，就像不吃鱼嘴里就不会有鱼腥味。
指不做坏事心里就踏实，做了坏事就会心虚。

bú zuò zhōng rén bú zuò bǎo yī shēng yī shì wú fán nǎo
不做中人不做保，一生一世无烦恼。

Proverb: Don't be a middleman or a guarantor, and your whole life will be without trouble.

Comment: If you assume responsibility for the behavior of others, they will bring you problems.

bú
不：no, not

zuò
做：do, be

zhōng
中：middle

rén
人：people

zhōng rén
中人：a middle man

bǎo
保：guarantee

bǎo rén
保人：a guarantor

bú zuò zhōng rén bú zuò bǎo
不做中人不做保：not be a middle man; not be a guarantor

yī
一：one

shēng shēng mìng
生 = 生命：life

shì
世：life time

yī shēng yī shì
一生一世：whole life

wú
无：without

fán nǎo
烦恼：trouble

yī shēng yī shì wú fán nǎo
一生一世无烦恼：your whole life will be without trouble

中人：中间人，见证人，调解人。保：担保人，推荐人。
不做中人和保人，就可以为自己省去许多麻烦。

cāng yīng bù dīng wú fèng dē dàn
苍 蝇 不 叮 无 缝 的 蛋。

Proverb: A fly doesn't suck an egg with no crack.

Comment: A person who behaves well will not be attacked by others.

cāng yīng
苍 蝇：a fly

bù
不：no, not

dīng
叮：suck

wú
无：without

fèng
缝：crack

wú fèng
无 缝：no crack

dē
的：'s

dàn
蛋：egg

wú fèng de dàn
无 缝 的 蛋：no crack egg

cāng yīng bù dīng wú fèng de dàn
苍 蝇 不 叮 无 缝 的 蛋：a fly doesn't suck an egg with no crack

如果鸡蛋没有裂缝，苍蝇便不会叮它。比喻人如果自身没有不端行为或可疑之处，别人就钻不了空子（本身如无懈可击，别人就奈何不了他）。

ceng jing cang hai nan wei shui chu que wu shan bu shi yun
曾 经 沧 海 难 为 水，除 却 巫 山 不 是 云。

Proverb: Once you see the dark blue sea, no other water is water; once you see the Wu Mountain's cloud, no other cloud is a cloud.

Comment: Wu Mountain, the east side of Chongqing Municipality of China, is the only route to visit the Three Gorges of the Yangtze River. According to an ancient myth, the goddess of clouds and rain is part of the Wu Mountain cloud.

céng jīng
曾 经：once

cāng
沧：dark blue

hǎi
海：sea

céng jīng cāng hǎi
曾 经 沧 海：once you see the dark blue sea

nán
难：difficult

wéi
为：become

shuǐ
水：water

céng jīng cāng hǎi nán wéi shuǐ
曾 经 沧 海 难 为 水：once you see the dark blue sea, no other water is water

chú què
除 却：without

wú shān
巫 山：the Wu mountain; also means Wu's cloud

bú
不：no, not

shì
是：is

yún
云：cloud

chú què wú shān bú shì yún
除 却 巫 山 不 是 云：once you see the Wu Mountain's cloud, no other cloud is a cloud

曾经经历过大海的广阔无边，不会再被别的水所吸引，巫山的云特别漂亮，走出了巫山，其他地方的云彩都称不上云彩了。指以前见过大场面的人，就不会把一般的东西放在眼里了。

肅靜
迴避
朝中有人好做官

cháo zhōng yǒu rén hǎo zhò guān
朝 中 有 人 好 做 官。

Proverb: If you have people in the government, it will be much easier to secure an official position.

Comment: Having a relationship, such as that with a close friend or a blood relative, will get things done much more easily.

cháo cháo tíng
朝 = 朝 廷：the government in traditional China

zhōng
中：in, inside

cháo zhōng
朝 中：in the goverment

yǒu
有：have, has

rén
人：people

yǒu rén
有 人 ：have close blood relatives or close friends

hǎo
好：good, fine

zuò
做：do, here means be

hǎo zuò
好 做：easy to be

guān
官：a government official

hǎo zuò guān
好 做 官：easier to secure an official position

有血缘关系的亲属和知音好朋友在朝廷当官，有这样背景的人就容易当官。指找有后台的人办事要容易得多。

chī fàn shǎo yī kǒu shuì jiào bù méng shǒu
吃 饭 少 一 口，睡 觉 不 蒙 首，

lǎo pó zhǎng dē chǒu bǎo nǐ huó dào jiǔ shí jiǔ
老婆 长 得 丑，保 你 活 到 九 十 九。

Proverb: When you eat a meal, have one bite less; when you are sleeping, don't cover up your head; when your wife is ugly, it is guaranteed you will live to be ninety-nine.
Comment: The Chinese traditionally believed that a man's having less sex would help him to live longer.

chī
吃：eat

fàn
饭：rice

chī fàn
吃 饭：have a meal

shǎo
少：less

yī
一：one

kǒu
口：mouth

yī kǒu
一 口：one bite

shǎo yī kǒu
少 一 口：one bite less

chī fàn shǎo yī kǒu
吃 饭 少 一 口：when you eat a meal, have one bite less

shuì jiào
睡 觉：sleep

bù
不：no, not

méng
蒙：cover up.

shǒu
首：the head

méng shǒu
蒙 首：cover up the head

shuì jiào bù méng shǒu
睡 觉 不 蒙 首：when sleeping, don't cover up the head

lǎo pó
老 婆：wife

zhǎng
长：grow

dē
得：no meaning, use after a verb to indicate can

chǒu
丑：ugly

zhǎng dē chǒu
长 得 丑：has an ugly looking

lǎo pó zhǎng dē chǒu
老 婆 长 得 丑：wife is ugly

bǎo bǎo zhèng
保 = 保 证：guarantee

nǐ
你：you

bǎo nǐ
保 你：guarantee you

huó
活：live

dào
到：up to, until

jiǔ
九：nine

shí
十：ten

jiǔ shí jiǔ
九 十 九：ninty nine, here means ninty-nine years old

bǎo nǐ huó dào jiǔ shí jiǔ
保 你 活 到 九 十 九：guarantee you will live until ninty-nine

指吃饭注意适量，睡觉被子不蒙头，不淫于色，就能长寿。

城门失火
殃及池鱼

chéng mén shī huǒ yāng jí chí yú
城门失火，殃及池鱼。

Proverb: The door on the city wall is on fire, bringing disaster to the fish in the moat.
Comment: Being associated with a person who has a problem can be a problem for you.

chéng
城：city

mén
门：door

chéng mén
城门：the door on the city wall

shī
失：lose, fail

huǒ
火：fire

shī huǒ
失火：on fire

chéng mén shī huǒ
城门失火：door on the city wall is on fire

yāng
殃：suffer dister

jí
及：reach

yāng jí
殃及：bring disaster to

chí
池：a pond, here means moat

yú
鱼：fish

yāng jí chí yú
殃及池鱼：bring disaster to the fish in the moat

城门失火，因取鱼池中的水救火，将池水汲干，鱼都渴死。比喻本来两不相干的事，无端受牵连而遭祸害。

cháng zǒu yè lù bì dìng yù jiàn guǐ
常 走 夜 路 必 定 遇 见 鬼。

Proverb: If you always walk on the road late at night, you will be sure to meet a ghost.
Comment: If you do bad things often, sooner or later, you will be punished.

cháng jīng cháng
常 = 经 常：always

zǒu
走：walk

yè
夜：night or evening

lù
路：a pass, a road

zǒu lù
走 路：walk

zǒu yè lù
走 夜 路：walk on the road late at night

cháng zǒu yè lù
常 走 夜 路：always walk on the road late at night

bì bì dìng
必 = 必 定：be sure

yù jiàn
遇 见：meet

guǐ
鬼：ghost, here means trouble

bì dìng yù jiàn guǐ
必 定 遇 见 鬼：be sure to meet a ghost

走夜路：指做见不得人的坏事。鬼：麻烦事，遭报应。指坏事不能多做，否则迟早遭到报应。

chéng shì bù sù bài shì yǒu yú
成 事 不 足，败 事 有 余。

Proverb: He has enough ability to damage things but not enough to accomplish things.

Comment: This is said to sneer at a totally hopeless idiot.

chéng wán chéng
成 = 完 成：accomplish

shì
事：thing, business

bù
不：no, not

bù zú
不 足：not enough

chéng shì bù zú
成 事 不 足：has not enough ability to accomplish things

bài
败：damage, spoil

bài shì
败 事：damage things

yǒu
有：have

yú
余：surplus, remainder

yǒu yú
有 余：have a surplus

bài shì yǒu yú
败 事 有 余：enough ability to damage things

办成事情的能力不够，把事情搞坏的本领却很强。用来嘲讽人，也用来提醒人与他们保持距离。

chī sù pèng dào yuè dà
吃 素 碰 到 月 大。

Proverb: A person decides to eat vegetarian for a month; unfortunately, this month has thirty-one days.

Comment: A person who is not really sincere in the beginning finds has to do more than he bargained for.

chī
吃：eat

sù sù cài
素 = 素 菜：vegetable

chī sù
吃 素：eat vegetarian

pèng dào
碰 到：by chance to run into

yuè
月：month

dà
大：biger, here means more

yuè dà
月 大：the month has one day more then other months

chī sù pèng dào yuè dà
吃 素 碰 到 月 大：eat vegetarian for a month, unfortunately this month has thirty one days

月小只有30天，遇到月大31天，就不得不多吃一天素。指本来就勉强去做的事，因为外界的原因，而不得不付出更大的努力继续做下去。

chī rén zuǐ duǎn ná rén shǒu ruǎn
吃 人 嘴 短， 拿 人 手 软。

Proverb: If you eat other people's food, you cannot criticize them; if you take something from people, you cannot punish them when they deserve it.
Comment: In this proverb, to eat or take something means to take bribes.

chī
吃：eat

rén
人：people, a person

chī rén
吃 人：eat somebody's food

zuǐ
嘴：mouth

duǎn
短：short

zuǐ duǎn
嘴 短：mouth is short; here means can't criticize

chī rén zuǐ duǎn
吃 人 嘴 短：If you eat other people's food, your short mouth cannot criticize them

ná
拿：take

ná rén
拿 人：take something from somebody

shǒu
手：hand

ruǎn
软：soft

shǒu ruǎn
手 软：your hand is soft

ná rén shǒu ruǎn
拿人 手 软：if you take something from people, your soft hand cannot punish them

吃了人家的东西，用了人家的钱财，腰杆子就硬不起来了。指受了人家的贿赂，遇事只得迁就，听从。建议不要去沾人家的小便宜。

chì jiǎo dē bú pà chuān xié dē
赤 脚 的 不 怕 穿 鞋 的。

Proverb: Barefoot people are not afraid of people who wear shoes.

Comment: Poor people have nothing to lose. Don't stir up trouble with them.

chì chì luǒ
赤 = 赤 裸：naked

jiǎo
脚：feet

chì jiǎo
赤 脚：barefoot

dē
的：'s

chì jiǎo dē
赤 脚 的：barefoot people; here means poor people

bú
不：no, not

pà
怕：fear, afraid

bú pà
不 怕：not afraid

chuān
穿：wear

xié
鞋：shoes

chuān xié dē
穿 鞋 的：people who wear shoes, indicates rich people

赤脚的：指穷人。穿鞋的：指有钱人。穷人一无所有，和富人抗争时无所顾忌。而富人却因为害怕失去很多，所以不敢和对方拼命。

chū shēng niú dú bú pà hǔ

初 生 牛 犊 不 怕 虎。

Proverb: A newborn calf is not afraid of the tiger.

Comment: Young people lack experience and don't know what is dangerous.

chū
初：in the early part of, at the beginning of

shēng chū shēng
生 = 出 生：born

chū shēng
初 生：a newborn

niú
牛：cow

dú
犊：baby cow

niú dú
牛 犊：calf

chū shēng niú dú
初 生 牛 犊：a newborn calf

bú
不：no, not

pà
怕：afraid

bú pà
不 怕：not afraid

hǔ
虎： tiger

bú pà hǔ
不 怕 虎：not afraid of the tiger

牛犊：小牛。刚生的小牛不怕虎。比喻阅历不深、缺少经验的年轻人不知道有什么可怕的，因此才敢作敢为，无所畏惧。

人财两旺
丑媳妇迟早要见公婆
張

chǒu xí fù chí zǎo yào jiàn gōng pó
丑 媳 妇 迟 早 要 见 公 婆。

Proverb: An ugly daughter-in-law has to meet her husband's parents sooner or later.
Comment: People can't hide their mistakes forever.

chǒu
丑：ugly

xí fù
媳 妇：daughter-in-law

chí
迟：late

zǎo
早：early

chí zǎo
迟 早：sooner or later

yào
要：want; here means have to

chí zǎo yào
迟 早 要：sooner or later have to

jiàn
见：see; here means meet

gōng gōng gōng
公 = 公 公：husband's father, father-in-law

pó pó pó
婆 = 婆 婆：husband's mother, mother-in-law

chí zǎo yào jiàn gōng pó
迟 早 要 见 公 婆：sooner or later have to meet father-in-law and mother-in-law

儿媳要伺候公婆，长得再丑迟早也要见面。比喻因某种原因犯了错误的人，迟早会被别人察觉，不可能总是躲避起来。

cóng jiǎn rù shē yì cóng shē rù jiǎn nán
从 俭 入 奢 易，从 奢 入 俭 难。

Proverb: Changing from a thrifty lifestyle to one of luxury is easy; changing from a life of luxury to one of thrift is difficult.
Comment: To go from poor to rich is an easy adjustment. To go from rich to poor is hard.

cóng
从：from, since

jiǎn jié jiǎn
俭 = 节 俭：a thrifty life style

rù
入：enter

shē shē chǐ
奢 = 奢 侈：a luxurious lifestyle

yì róng yì
易 = 容 易：easy

cóng jiǎn rù shē yì
从 俭 入 奢 易：changing from a thrifty lifestyle to one of luxury is easy

nán
难：difficult

cóng shē rù jiǎn nán
从 奢 入 俭 难：changing from a life of luxury to one of thrift is difficult

指从过穷日子到过奢侈的日子容易，过惯了好日子再过穷日子就难了。劝人在有钱时不要太铺张浪费。

dǎ rén xiū dǎ liǎn mà rén xiū jiē duǎn
打 人 休 打 脸，骂 人 休 揭 短。

Proverb: When you hit someone, do not hit his face; when you yell at somebody, do not reveal his shortcomings.
Comment: Even when you hurt someone's feelings, don't overdo it.

dǎ
打：hit, beat

rén
人：a person, people

dǎ rén
打 人：hit people

xiū bú yào
休 = 不 要：do not

liǎn
脸：face

dǎ liǎn
打 脸：hit the face

dǎ rén xiū dǎ liǎn
打人 休 打 脸：when you hit someone, do not hit his face

mà
骂：scold, yell

mà rén
骂 人：yell at someone

jiē
揭：reveal

duǎn
短：short, shortcoming

mà rén xiū jiē duǎn
骂 人 休揭 短：when you yell at someone, do not reveal his shortcomings

指争斗中，就像在打架时不要打人的脸一样，争吵时骂人也不要揭人的短处，不要太伤害对方，要给人留些脸面。

打狗要看主人面

dǎ gǒu yào kàn zhǔ rén miàn
打 狗 要 看 主 人 面。

Proverb: Before you beat a dog, consider its master's face.
Comment: Before you punish somebody, you have to consider who is behind that person. "Face" here refers to the importance of the master and not giving offense to an important person.

dǎ
打：hit, beat, here means punish

gǒu
狗：dog

yào
要：want, have to

kàn
看：see, look at; here means consider

zhǔ rén
主 人：master

miàn miàn zǐ
面 = 面 子：face

dǎ gǒu yào kàn zhǔ rén miàn
打 狗 要 看 主 人 面：before you beat a dog, consider its master's face

比喻在惩处某一个人时，要顾及其主子或与其关系密切的人的情面，不能不权衡轻重。

打虎亲兄弟 上阵父子兵
張林

dǎ hǔ qīn xiōng dì shàng zhèn fù zǐ bīng
打 虎 亲 兄 弟，上 阵 父 子 兵。

Proverb: To hunt for a tiger, you should have blood brothers with you; to go into battle, comrades should be father and son.

Comment: In facing a high risk situation , you should have people with you that you can trust. Traditionally, Chinese placed the most trust in members of their own family.

dǎ
打：hit, here means hunt

hǔ
虎：tiger

dǎ hǔ
打 虎：hunt for a tiger; here means a kinds of high risk business

qīn
亲：close, blood relation

xiōng dì
兄 弟：brother

qīn xiōng dì
亲 兄 弟：blood brothers

shàng zhèn
上 阵：go into battle

fù
父：father子：son

zǐ
子

bīng
兵：soldier

fù zǐ bīng
父 子 兵：comrades father and son

指在做上山打虎或上阵杀敌等危及生命的事情时，只有情如父子和亲如兄弟的人，才能做到同心协力去完成。

dǎ zhǒng liǎn chōng pàng zi
打 肿 脸 充 胖 子。

Proverb: Slap your face until it is swollen and then pretend you are fat.
Comment: People try to pretend they are stronger or better than they are. Traditionally, only rich people were fat. Being fat denoted status.

dǎ
打：hit, beat, slap

zhǒng
肿：swollen

liǎn
脸：face

dǎ zhǒng liǎn
打 肿 脸：slap face until it's swollen

chōng mào chōng
充 = 冒 充：pretend

pàng zi
胖 子：a fat person

chōng pàng zi
充 胖 子：pretend to be a fat person

dǎ zhǒng liǎn chōng pàng zi
打 肿 脸 充 胖 子：slap your face until it's swollen and then pretend you are fat

充：冒充。比喻在没有实力的情况下，硬充好汉，装门面摆架子。

dà shì huà xiǎo xiǎo shì huà liǎo
大 事 化 小，小 事 化 了。

Proverb: Reduce a big problem into small problems; then let the small problems fade away.

Comment: One way not to be overwhelmed by a complicated problem is to break it down into its parts and then wait until the small problems disappear.

dà
大：big, large

shì
事：thing; here means problem

dà shì
大 事：a big problem

huà huà jiě
化 = 化 解：change, reduce

xiǎo
小：small, little

xiǎo shì
小 事：a big problem

dà shì huà xiǎo
大 事 化 小：reduce a big problem into a small problem

xiǎo shì
小 事：a small problem

liǎo liǎo jié
了 = 了 结：finish, end; here means fade away

xiǎo shì huà liǎo
小 事 化 了：make the small problem fade away

这是处理问题的一种方法，就是淡化矛盾，这样大的矛盾就缩小了，到最后连小矛盾也不用解决，把小事变成了没事一般。

dà shù dǐ xià hǎo chéng liáng
大树底下好乘凉。

Proverb: The shade of the big tree offers a cool place to relax.

Comment: Having powerful people's protection will make things easier.

dà
大：big, large

shù
树：tree

dǐ xià
底下：below, under

dà shù dǐ xià
大树底下：under the big tree; here means under the shade of the big tree

hǎo
好：good, fine; here means cool

chéng liáng
乘凉：relax in a cool place

hǎo chéng liáng
好乘凉：a cool place to relax

dà shù dǐ xià hǎo chéng liáng
大树底下好乘凉：the shade of the big tree offers a cool place to relax

树大，遮阴的面积大，树下好乘凉。常比喻有势力大的靠山就好办事。

dà shuǐ chōng lē lóng wáng miào
大 水 冲 了 龙 王 庙，

yī jiā rén bú rèn dé yī jiā rén
一 家 人 不 认 得 一 家 人。

Proverb: Water floods the dragon's temple; people in the same family do not recognize each other.

Comment: The "family" is the dragon, the temple, and the water. The dragon is the god of water. People say this proverb to show that misunderstanding happens among people in the same group.

dà 大：big　shuǐ 水：water　dà shuǐ 大水：flood　chōng 冲：flood away

lē 了：no meaning, used after a verb to show change already finished

lóng 龙：dragon　wáng 王：king　miào 庙：temple　lóng wáng miào 龙王庙：dragon temple

dà shuǐ chōng lē lóng wáng miào 大水冲了龙王庙：water floods the dragon's temple

yī 一：one　jiā 家：family　rén 人：people

yī jiā rén 一家人：people in the same family　bú 不：no, not　rèn dé 认得：recognize

yī jiā rén bú rèn dé yī jiā rén 一家人不认得一家人：people in the same family do not recognize each other

龙王是水神，龙王庙是祭奉龙王的地方，大水把龙王庙冲坏了，是大水不认识龙王庙的结果。指自己人之间发生误会。

dà yú chī xiǎo yú xiǎo yú chī xiā mǐ
大鱼吃小鱼，小鱼吃虾米。

Proverb: Big fish eat small fish; small fish eat shrimp.

Comment: In the real world, the big and strong always bully and humiliate the small and weak.

dà
大：big, large

xiǎo
小：small, little

yú
鱼：fish

dà yú
大鱼：big fish

xiǎo yú
小鱼：small fish

chī
吃：eat

dà yú chī xiǎo yú
大鱼吃小鱼：big fish eat small fish

xiā mǐ
虾米：shrimp

xiǎo yú chī xiā mǐ
小鱼吃虾米：small fish eat shrimp

虾米：小虾。比喻强的、大的总是欺凌弱的、小的。

dāng guān dē dòng dòng zuǐ dāng bīng dē pǎo duàn tuǐ
当 官 的 动 动 嘴，当 兵 的 跑 断 腿。

Proverb: The official moves his lips to command; the soldier runs and breaks his leg.

Comment: This saying is used to complain about having a rough time.

dāng
当：be

guān
官：a goverment official

dē
的：'s

dāng guān dē
当 官 的：a person who is an official

dòng
动：make a movement

zuǐ
嘴：mouth

dòng dòng zuǐ
动 动 嘴：move the lips; here means talk and give orders

dāng guān dē dòng dòng zuǐ
当 官 的 动 动 嘴：when the official moves his lips to command

bīng
兵：soldier

dāng bīng dē
当 兵 的：a person who is a soldier

pǎo
跑：run

duàn
断：break

tuǐ
腿：leg

dāng bīng dē pǎo duàn tuǐ
当 兵 的 跑 断 腿：soldier runs and breaks his leg

官老爷下一个命令，下面的人就忙得半死。用于抱怨吃苦受累。

当局者迷 旁观者清
張芷

dāng jú zhě mí páng guān zhě qīng
当局者迷，旁观者清。

Proverb: The chess players are confused; the spectators see the game better than the players.

Comment: Outsiders can see things better than those involved.

dāng jú
当局：the authority

zhě
者：a person or people

dāng jú zhě
当局者：the authority; here means the chess player

mí = mí huò
迷 = 迷惑：be confused

dāng jú zhě mí
当局者迷：the player is confused

páng = páng biān
旁 = 旁边：by the side of

guān = guān kàn
观 = 观看：look at

páng guān zhě
旁观者：spectator

qīng = qīng chǔ
清 = 清楚：clear

páng guān zhě qīng
旁观者清：the spectator see the game better than the players

下棋的人往往对局势认识不清，而在一旁观看的人却比较清楚。也指当事人往往失去正确的判断能力，而局外人反而比较清醒。

dāng jiā shì gè nián qíng láng cān cān wō tóu xīn bù liáng
当家是个年轻郎，餐餐窝头心不凉。

Proverb: The master of the family is a young man; at every meal, his wife eats wo tou and still is perfectly happy.

Comment: Wo Tou is poor people's food. It is steamed rice bran.

jiā
家：home

dāng jiā
当家：the master of the family

shì
是：is

gè
个：a measure word for people

shì gè
是个：is a

nián qīng
年轻：young

láng
郎：a man

dāng jiā shì gè nián qīng láng
当家是个年轻郎：the master of the family is a young man

cān
餐：a meal

cān cān
餐餐：every meal

wō tóu
窝头：Wo Tou, poor people's food, stramed by rice bran

xīn
心：heart

bù
不：not

liáng
凉：cool

cān cān wō tóu xīn bù liáng
餐餐窝头心不凉：even though at every meal his wife eats Wo Tou, she still is perfectly happy

当家：家里的主人，这里指丈夫。窝头是粗粮做的，指艰苦的生活条件。嫁了个年轻力壮的丈夫，即便跟他过苦日子也心甘情愿。

dāng zhē hé shàng mà zéi tū
当 着 和 尚 骂 贼 秃。

Proverb: In the presence of a monk, he shouts "bald-headed thief" at another person.

Comment: Monks have shaved heads. Shouting "bald-headed thief" at another person is really a way to insult the monk. This proverb might be used to insult a powerful person indirectly by insulting someone else.

dāng zhē
当 着：in the presence of

hé shàng
和 尚：a monk

dāng zhē hé shàng
当 着 和 尚：in the presence of a monk

mà
骂：shout

zéi
贼：thief

tū
秃：a bald head

zéi tū
贼 秃：bald-headed thief

mà zéi tū
骂 贼 秃：he shouts "bald-headed thief"

贼秃：是骂人的话。当着和尚的面骂另一个人是秃子，看似骂别人，实际上是在骂和尚。比喻明指着骂某个人，实际上暗骂另一个人。

dí qiáng yòng zhì dí ruò yòng shì
敌 强 用 智，敌 弱 用 势。

Proverb: When the enemy is big and powerful, use wisdom to deal with them; when the enemy is weak, use power.
Comment: Outsmarting a powerful opponent has always been part of the Chinese tradition. Power can be used to threaten weaker opponents.

dí
敌：an enemy

qiáng
强：big and powerful

yòng
用：use

zhì zhì huì
智 = 智 慧：wisdom

dí qiáng yòng zhì
敌 强 用 智：when the enemy is big and powerful, use wisdom to deal with

ruò
弱：weak

shì
势：power

yòng shì
用 势：use power

dí ruò yòng shì
敌 弱 用 势：when the enemy is weak, use power

智：智谋。势：威势。对付强敌要用智谋去应付，对付弱敌，要用威势来压制他。

diāo sù jiàng bù gěi shén xiàng kòu tóu zhī dào lǎo dǐ
雕塑匠不给神像叩头—知道老底。

Proverb: The sculptor doesn't kowtow to the sculpture of the deity because he knows the inside story.

Comment: The sculpture was made from mud and wood by the sculptor. A person in the know, such as the sculptor, will not be fooled.

diāo sù
雕 塑：sculpture

jiàng
匠：a craftsman

diāo sù jiàng
雕 塑 匠：sculptor

bù
不：no, not

gěi
给：give

shén
神：deity

shén xiàng
神 像：sculpture of a deity

kòu tóu
叩 头：kowtow

diāo sù jiàng bù gěi shén xiàng kòu tóu
雕 塑 匠 不给 神 像 叩 头：the sculptor doesn't kowtow to the sculpture of deity

zhī dào
知 道：know

lǎo dǐ
老 底：the inside story

zhī dào lǎo dǐ
知 道 老 底：he knows the inside story

不叩头是因为知道神像是用泥巴和木头雕塑而成。比喻知情人不会上当。

diē yǒu bù rú niáng yǒu niáng yǒu bù rú lǎo pó yǒu
爹有不如娘有，娘有不如老婆有，

lǎo pó yǒu hái yào kāi kāi kǒu bù rú zì jǐ yǒu
老婆有还要开开口，不如自己有。

Proverb: When a man's father has the money, it is not as good as his mother having it. When the mother has it, it's not as good as his wife having it; he still has to open his mouth to ask his wife for it. It is better to have the money himself.

Comment: Obviously direct control over important things like money is better than indirect.

diē
爹：father

yǒu
有：have

diē yǒu
爹有：father has money

bù rú
不如：not as good as

niáng
娘：mother

niáng yǒu
娘有：mother has money

lǎo pó
老婆：wife

lǎo pó yǒu
老婆有：wife has money

hái
还：still

yào
要：have to

kāi
开：open

kǒu
口：mouth

kāi kāi kǒu kāi kǒu
开开口=开口：open mouth to ask

zì jǐ
自己：self

bù rú zì jǐ yǒu
不如自己有：better to have the money himself

娘比爹好说话，老婆又比娘更好商量，但还是自己有钱用起来更方便。
指父母的财富再多，也不如自己拥有，要过好日子，只能靠自己。

diū lē guǎi zhàng jiù shòu gǒu qì
丢 了 拐 杖 就 受 狗 气。

Proverb: Once you throw down your stick, you are going to be bullied by a dog.
Comment: If you have no ability to protect yourself, anyone can humiliate you.

diū
丢：throw down

lē
了：no meaning, used after a verb to show the action already finished

guǎi zhàng
拐 仗：a stick, here means a weapon for self-defence

jiù jiù yào
就 = 就 要：going to

shòu qì
受……气：be bullied by somebody or something

gǒu
狗：dog

shòu gǒu qì
受 狗 气：bullied by a dog

diū lē guǎi zhàng jiù shòu gǒu qì
丢了拐 仗就受 狗气：once you throw down your stick, you are going to be bullied by a dog

人如果不懂得或者是没有本领保护自己，谁都会来欺负你。

洞房花烛夜
金榜题名时

dòng fáng huā zhú yè jīn bǎng tí míng shí
洞 房 花 烛 夜，金 榜 题 名 时。

Proverb: Nothing compares with the pleasures of the wedding night and the moment of the yellow-colored board's announcement of who succeeded in the government examination.
Comment: These were the two most exciting moments in an intellectual's life in ancient China. People say this proverb when they are extremely proud. The "pleasures of the wedding night" does not need an explanation. "The moment of the yellow-colored board's announcement" refers to the results of the Imperial examinations which determined an intellectual's future in traditional China. The examinations were instituted in the Sui Dynasty(581-681) and were expanded further in later dynasties. The exams were only open to men.

dòng
洞：hole

fáng
房：house

dòng fáng
洞 房：a bridal chamber

huā
花：flower

zhú
烛：candle

huā zhú
花 烛：rad candle use for wedding

yè
夜：night

dòng fáng huā zhú yè
洞 房 花 烛 夜：the night of wedding night

jīn
金：golden

jīn bǎng
金 榜：yellow-colored board to announce winner's nname

tí
题：an autograph

míng
名：name

shí
时：time, the moment

jīn bǎng tí míng shí
金 榜 题 名 时：the moment of the yellow-colored board's announcement of who succeeded in a government examination

洞房花烛夜：新婚之夜。金榜题名：古时科举时代考试得中，公布录取姓名于黄榜上。这两件事是人生最得意的事情。指一种洋洋得意的心态。

duì kè bù dé chén gǒu
对客不得嗔狗。

Proverb: In front of guests, you should not berate the dog.
Comment: The guests will feel that by berating the dog, the person is showing disrespect to them.

duì duì dài
对 = 对待：deal with

kè kè rén
客 = 客人：a visitor, a guest

duì kè
对客：deal with a guest

bù
不：no, not

bù dé
不得：can not; here means not allowed

chén
嗔：berate

gǒu
狗：a dog

chén gǒu
嗔狗：berate the dog

duì kè bù dé chén gǒu
对客不得嗔狗：in front of guests, you should not berate the dog

嗔：发怒，生气，指呵责。当着客人的面不能呵斥狗。指待客要有礼貌，避免引起不必要的误会。

duō	nián	dē	xiǎo	dào	liú	chéng	hé
多	年	的	小	道	流	成	河，
duō	nián	dē	xí	fù	áo	chéng	pó
多	年	的	媳	妇	熬	成	婆。

Expression: For many years a small stream flows in a narrow path and then becomes a river; a daughter-in-law is tortured many years (by her mother-in-law), but sooner or later she will become a mother-in-law.

Meaning: A way of comforting people! Once a daughter-in-law becomes a mother-in-law, it will be her turn to torture her daughter-in-law.

duō
多：many, more

nián
年：year

dē
的：'s

xiǎo dào
小 道：a narrow path

liú
流：flow

chéng
成：become

hé
河：a river

duō nián dē xiǎo diào liú chéng hé
多 年 的 小 道 流 成 河：for many years a small stream flows in a narrow path and then becomes a river

xí fù
媳 妇：daughter-in-law

áo
熬：is tortured

pó
婆：mother-in-law

duō nián dē xí fù áo chéng pó
多 年 的 媳 妇 熬 成 婆：a daughter-in-law is tortured many years (by her mother-in-law), but sooner or later she will become a mother-in-law

指小路一旦积水，时间一长就成了河。媳妇虽然要受婆婆的气，时间一长，媳妇迟早也会变成婆婆，给她的儿媳妇受气了。

duō qíng zhě bì hào sè hào sè zhě wèi bì duō qíng
多 情 者必好 色，好 色 者 未必多 情。

Proverb: If a man has a lot of love, he definitely will be full of lust. But a man who has lust may not necessarily have love.

Comment: Love for a man will include sex. But with a man sex by itself will not always produce love.

duō qíng
多 情：has a lot of love

zhě
者：a person, people

duō qíng zhě
多 情 者：a person has a lot of love

bì　bì dìng
必 = 必 定：definitely

hào sè
好 色：lust for women

duō qíng zhě bì hào sè
多 情 者 必 好 色：If a man has a lot of love, he definitely will be full of lust

wèi bì
未 必：not necessarily

hào sè zhě wèi bì duō qíng
好 色 者 未 必 多 情：a man who has lust may not necessarily have love

重感情的人必定喜爱美色，而喜爱美色的人却不一定重感情。

ér bù xián mǔ chǒu gǒu bù xián jiā pín
儿不嫌母丑，狗不嫌家贫。

Proverb: A son never deserts his mother because of her ugly face; a dog won't forsake his master because the master is poor.

Comment: Chinese say this to their children to instill gratitude for their upbringing and to teach them not to abandon their parents.

ér
儿：son

bù
不：no, not

xián xián qì
嫌 = 嫌 弃：forsake, desert

mǔ mǔ qīn
母 = 母 亲：mother

chǒu
丑：ugly

ér bù xián mǔ chǒu
儿不嫌母丑：son never deserts his mother for her ugly face

gǒu
狗：dog

jiā
家：home

pín pín qióng
贫 = 贫 穷：poor

jiā pín
家 贫：poor home; here means poor master

gǒu bù xián jiā pín
狗不嫌家贫：dog won't forsake his master because the master is poor

这是中国人的道德理念，子女要感激父母的养育之恩，就像狗始终如一地忠实于它的主人一样。

ér sūn zì yǒu ér sūn fú mò wèi ér sūn dāng mǎ niú
儿孙自有儿孙福，莫为儿孙当马牛。

Proverb: Later generations have their own fortune; don't become a horse and cow for them.

Comment: Don't be a slave for future generations.

ér
儿：son

sūn
孙：grandson

ér sūn
儿孙：later generations

zì zì jǐ
自 = 自己：self

yǒu
有：have

fú
福：fortune

ér sūn zì yǒu ér sūn fú
儿孙自有儿孙福：later generations have their own fortune

mò
莫：don't

wèi
为：for

dāng
当：be, become

mǎ
马：horse

niú
牛：cow

mò wèi ér sūn dāng mǎ niú
莫为儿孙当马牛：don't become a horse and cow for them

指子孙后代自有他们的福运，做长辈的不必为他们过分操劳。

fǎ chǎng shàng dē má què dǎn zi zǎo xià dà le
法 场 上 的 麻 雀，胆 子 早 吓 大 了。

Proverb: The sparrows that live in the execution grounds have more courage because they have been scared before.
Comment: People who have gone through dangerous situations are more brave.

fǎ chǎng xíng chǎng
法 场 = 刑 场：the execution grounds

shàng
上：on top of, up, above

dē
的：'s

má què
麻 雀：a sparrow

fǎ chǎng shàng dē má què
法 场 上 的 麻 雀：the sparrow that lives in the execution grounds

dǎn zi
胆 子：courage

zǎo
早：early, before

xià
吓：threaten, scare

dà
大：big

le
了：no meaning, used after a verb to show change already finished

dǎn zi zǎo xià dà le
胆 子 早 吓 大 了：have more courage because they have been scared before

法场：刑场。比喻经历的险境多，胆子大。

fān shǒu wéi yún fù shǒu wéi yǔ
翻 手 为 云，覆 手 为 雨。

Proverb: Turn the palm up, and a cloud comes out; turn the palm down, and a cloud becomes rain.

Comment: This proverb describes a powerful politician.

fān
翻：turn over

shǒu
手：hand

fān shǒu
翻 手：turn the palm up

wéi
为：become

yún
云：cloud

wéi yún
为 云：become a cloud

fān shǒu wéi yún
翻 手 为 云：turns the palm up, a cloud comes out

fù
覆：turn down

fù shǒu
覆 手：turn the palm down

yǔ
雨：rain

wéi yǔ
为 雨：become rain

fù shǒu wéi yǔ
覆 手 为 雨：turns the palm down, a cloud becomes rain

云能化成雨，用将云雨变来变去来形容某些人喜好玩弄权术，做事反复无常，而且神通广大，掀起一场场风波。

fàng xià tú dāo lì dì chéng fó
放 下 屠 刀，立 地 成 佛。

Proverb: A butcher immediately becomes a Buddha when he drops his cleaver.

Comment: This is the saying whereby Buddhism advises evil people to reform themselves.

fàng
放：put down, drop

xià
下：below, down

tú
屠：kill or massacre

dāo
刀：knife, cleaver

tú dāo
屠 刀：a butcher's knife, a cleaver

lì dì
立 地：immediately

chéng
成：become

fó
佛：Buddha

fàng xià tú dāo lì dì chéng fó
放 下 屠 刀，立 地 成 佛：a butcher immediately becomes a Buddha when he drops his cleaver

屠刀：杀人或宰杀畜牲。这是佛家劝人改恶从善的话。比喻作恶的人一旦认识了自己的罪行，决心改过，仍可以很快变成好人。

fēi niǎo jìn liáng gōng cáng jiǎo tù sǐ zǒu gǒu pēng
飞鸟尽，良 弓 藏；狡兔死，走 狗 烹；

dí guó pò móu chén wáng
敌国破，谋 臣 亡。

Proverb: When the birds are all killed, hide the excellent bow; when the rabbits are all dead, cook the hunting dog; when the enemy country has been defeated, execute the wartime officials.
Comment: This was the famous policy of Ming (1368-1644) dynasty emperor Zhu Yuan Zhang. After first taking power, he executed those who had made great contributions to his taking power. Otherwise, they may have tried to claim credit for themselves and to take over from him.

fēi
飞：fly

niǎo
鸟：a bird

jìn
尽：finished

fēi niǎo jìn
飞 鸟 尽：birds are all killed

liáng
良：excellent

gōng
弓：a bow

cáng
藏：hide

liáng gōng cáng
良 弓 藏：hide the excellent bow

jiǎo
狡：trick

tù
兔：rabbit

sǐ
死：die

jiǎo tù sǐ
狡 兔 死：rabbits all died

zǒu gǒu
走 狗：hunting dog

pēng pēng rèn
烹 = 烹 饪：cook

zǒu gǒu pēng
走 狗 烹：cook the hunting dogs

dí
敌：enemy

guó guó jiā
国 = 国 家：country

pò
破：break apart, defeat

dí guó pò
敌 国 破：enemy country has been defeated

móu
谋：a strategy

chén
臣：official in traditional China

móu chén
谋 臣：officials with great contributions

wáng
亡：die, kill, execute

móu chén wáng
谋 臣 亡：executed those who had made great contributions

尽：没有了，指杀光了。藏：指收起来不用了。走狗：猎狗。烹：煮，指杀掉吃了。破：打败。谋臣：指当年一起打天下的出谋划策的功臣。亡：清除掉。鸟杀光了，弓也用不上了，可以藏起来了；兔子都猎光了，狗就派不上用处，可以杀掉煮了吃了；夺取政权以后，当初一起打天下的功臣没有用了，还留着干什么，这些人可能还会居功抢权，倒不如杀了干净。这是指历史上刘邦和朱元璋搞的“天下初定，先杀功臣”的运动。

féi shuǐ bù liú tā rén tián
肥 水 不 流 他 人 田。

Proverb: Manure shouldn't go to other people's land.

Comment: If you can do something yourself, that's better. Otherwise, the profits will go to other people's pockets.

féi
肥：fat, rich

shuǐ
水：water

féi shuǐ
肥 水：manure; here means benefits

bù
不：no, not

liú
流：go, flow

tā qí tā
他 = 其 他：other

rén
人：a person, people

tā rén
他 人：other people

tián
田：farmland; here means pocket

féi shuǐ bù liú tā rén tián
肥 水 不 流 他 人 田：manure shouldn't go to other people's land

他人：外人。比喻便宜和好处是不能让外人分享的，要自己独得。

fēng mǎ niú bù xiāng jí
风 马 牛 不 相 及。

Proverb: There is no sexual interest between a horse and a cow.
Comment: This is said to describe two things that are totally unrelated.

fēng
风：wind, another meaning is sexual attraction in the animal world

mǎ
马：house

niú
牛：cow

fēng mǎ niú
风 马 牛：sexual interest between a house and a cow

bù
不：no, not

xiāng jí　xiāng gān
相 及 = 相 干：have to do with

bù xiāng jí
不 相 及：have nothing to do with

fēng mǎ niú bù xiāng jí
风 马 牛 不 相 及：no sexual interest between a horse and a cow

风：指动物雌雄相诱。不相及：毫不相干。马牛因不同的种族，是不可能发生性关系的。用来形容毫不相干的两件事。

fù mǔ zài bù yuǎn yóu yóu bì yǒu fān
父 母 在，不 远 游，游 必 有 方。

Proverb: When your parents are still alive, do not take a long trip; if you have to go, you must tell your parents where you are going.
Comment: An example of the Chinese sense of filial devotion.

fù
父：father

mǔ
母：mother

fù mǔ
父 母：parent

zài
在：exist, alive

fù mǔ zài
父 母 在：when parents alive

bù
不：no, not

yuǎn
远：far, long

yóu
游：swim; here means take a trip

bù yuǎn yóu
不 远 游：not take a long trip

bì
必：must, have to

yǒu
有：have

fāng fāng xiàng
方 = 方 向：direction

bì yǒu fāng
必 有 方：must tell the direction; here means where you are going

yóu bì yǒu fāng
游 必 有 方：If you have to go, you must tell your parents where you are going

在：在世，指活着。父母在世的时候，不应该出远门，如果一定要走，也必须告知父母你的去向，以免年老的父母因为心中无数而担心，牵挂。这是中国人小辈孝敬长辈的道理。

fù bú guò sān dài
富 不 过 三 代。

Proverb: Wealth cannot last three generations.
Comment: Wealthy families often will bring up spendthrifts and incompetents who will squander the families' wealth.

fù
富：wealthy, rich

bú
不：no, not

guò
过：carry on, last

bú guò
不过：cannot last

sān
三：three

dài
代：generation

sān dài
三代：three generations

fù bú guò sān dài
富不过三代：wealth cannot last three generations

富贵人家易出败家子，不出三代的时间，就把财富都挥霍干净，
不可能连续三代享受荣华富贵。

fù cháo zhī xià qǐ yǒu wán luǎn
覆 巢 之 下，岂 有 完 卵。

Proverb: If the nest is turned upside down, how can you find unbroken eggs?
Comment: If the whole thing collapses, nothing can survive.

fù
覆：turn upside down

cháo
巢：nest

fù cháo
覆 巢：the nest turned upside down

zhī
之：'s

xià
下：below, under, down

zhī xià
之 下：under the

fù cháo zhī xià
覆 巢 之 下：under the turned upside down nest

qǐ
岂：how can

yǒu
有：have, has

qǐ yǒu
岂 有：isn't have

wán wán zhěng dē
完 = 完 整 的：whole

luǎn
卵：an egg

wán luǎn
完 卵：an unbroken egg

qǐ yǒu wán luǎn
岂有 完 卵：how can you find an unbroken egg

翻倒在地的鸟巢里，不会再有完整的鸟蛋。比喻整体覆灭了，局部不可能幸免。

gé nián dē huáng lì bù guǎn yòng
隔 年 的 黄 历 不 管 用。

Proverb: Last year's imperial calendar is useless.

Comment: The emperor issued a yellow calendar every year. The Chinese calendar is lunisolar, combining elements of a solar and lunar calendar. Dates move under lunar calendars each year, unlike under an accurate solar calendar, where dates are fixed. Chinese New Year therefore falls on a different date each year. Supposedly the first Chinese calendar was invented under the legendary Emperor Huang Di (2697-2597 BCE).

gé
隔：separate

nián
年：year

dē
的：'s

gé niáng dē
隔 年 的：previous year's, last year's

huáng
黄：yellow

huáng lì
黄 历：a emperor issued a yellow lunar calendar

gé nián dē huáng lì
隔 年 的 黄 历：last year's emperor issued a yellow lunar calendar

bù
不：no, not

guǎn
管：control

yòng
用：use

guǎn yòng
管 用：useful

bù guǎn yòng
不 管 用：useless

黄历是旧时皇帝颁布的封面黄色的年历，一年一本，是根据每一年不同的二十四个时节而编排的供参考的守则，规定这一年农民该做什么，不该做什么。比喻形势变了，过期的老办法不灵了。

gé	zhē	bù	dài	mǎi	māo
隔	着	布	袋	买	猫。

Proverb: Buy a cat with the cat wrapped in a cotton bag.

Comment: The cat is in the bag, so the buyer cannot see the cat. Frequently used as a metaphor for a traditional marriage where the husband and wife did not see one another before the wedding.

gé
隔：separate, partition, here means wrapped in something

zhē
着：no meaning, indicate an action or status continued

bù
布：cotton

dài
袋：bag

bù dài
布 袋：cotton bag

gé zhē bù dài
隔 着 布 袋：wrapped in a cotton bag

mǎi
买：buy

māo
猫：cat

gé zhē bù dài mǎi māo
隔 着 布 袋 买 猫：buy a cat with the cat wrapped in a cotton bag

比喻没看过样品就定货，常指老式的包办婚姻。

gōng jìng mò rú cóng mìng shòu xùn mò rú cóng shùn
恭 敬 莫如 从 命，受 训 莫如 从 顺。

Proverb: Politeness is not as good as obeying an order; being scolded is not as good as being obedient.

Comment: This is in the Confucian tradition, which stresses obedience.

gōng gōng jìng
恭 = 恭 敬：respectful

mò rú bù rú
莫 如 = 不 如：not as good as

cóng shùn cóng
从 = 顺 从：be obedient

mìng mìng lìng
命 = 命 令：an order

cóng mìng
从 命：obeying an order, obedience

gōng jìng mò rú cóng mìng
恭 敬 莫 如 从 命：politeness is not as good as obeying an order

shòu
受：receive, accept

xùn xùn chì
训 = 训 斥：scold, lecture

shòu xùn
受 训：accept a scolding

shùn shùn cóng
顺 = 顺 从：be obedient

shòu xùn mò rú cóng shùn
受 训 莫 如 从 顺：being scolded is not as good as being obedient

与其一味恭敬礼让，不如听从对方的吩咐。与其受到训斥，不如顺从对方。常用来表示听从对方的吩咐，多用在接受别人恩惠时说的客套话。

关公面前舞大刀

guān gōng miàn qián wǔ dà dāo
关 公 面 前 舞 大 刀。

Proverb: Wave a big knife in front of Guan Gong.
Comment: Active during the late Eastern Han Dynasty, Guan Gong was a famous Chinese military general. He was known for using a big knife as a weapon. This proverb describes a person who shows off his abilities in front of someone who is much better than he.

guān gōng
关 公：a name

miàn qián
面 前：in front of

guān gōng miàn qián
关 公 面 前：in front of Guan Gong

wǔ = huī wǔ
舞 = 挥 舞：wave

dà
大：big

dāo
刀：a knife

wǔ dà dāo
舞 大 刀：wave a big knife

guān gōng miàn qián wǔ dà dāo
关 公 面 前 舞 大 刀：wave a big knife in front of Guan Gong

关公：中国历史上最有名的武将，他擅长使用的兵器是大刀。指在比自己强得多的人面前卖弄本事。

gǒu shòu mò tī mǎ bìng mò qí rén qióng mò qī
狗 瘦 莫踢，马 病 莫骑，人 穷 莫欺。

Proverb: Don't kick a thin dog; don't ride a sick horse; don't insult poor people.

Comment: Don't take advantage of or hurt weaker people. Remember they have nothing to lose if attacked.

gǒu
狗：dog

shòu
瘦：thin

mò bú yào
莫 = 不 要：don't

tī
踢：kick

gǒu shòu mò tī
狗 瘦 莫 踢：don't kick a thin dog

mǎ
马：horse

bìng
病：sick

qí
骑：ride

mǎ bìng mò qí
马 病 莫 骑：don't ride a sick horse

rén
人：people

qióng
穷：poor

qī
欺：insult, humiliate

rén qióng mò qī
人 穷 莫 欺：don't insult poor people

吃不饱的瘦狗本来火气就大，你再踢它一脚，它就很可能上来咬你一口，还是走开点的好。骑上病马，后果不可预料，说不定摔个半死，也是不值得的。欺负穷人也会惹得他跟你拼命，因为穷人是没有什么好损失的，打起来时是不要命的，最好不要招惹他。

guà yáng tóu mài gǒu ròu
挂 羊 头，卖 狗 肉。

Proverb: Displays a sheep's head, but sells dog meat.
Comment: Equivalent to the English expression "bait and switch."

guà
挂：hang up, display

yáng
羊：a sheep, a goat

tóu
头：head

yáng tóu
羊 头：a sheep's head

guà yáng tóu
挂 羊 头：display a sheep's head

mài
卖：sell

gǒu
狗：dog

ròu
肉：meat

gǒu ròu
狗 肉：dog meat

mài gǒu ròu
卖 狗 肉：sell dog meat

guà yáng tóu mài gǒu ròu
挂 羊 头 卖 狗 肉：display a sheep's head, but sell dog meat

指名不符其实。也指说的是一套，做的是另一套。

guān cái lǐ shēn chū shǒu lái sǐ yào qián
棺 材 里 伸 出 手 来 — 死 要 钱。

Proverb: The hand sticks out from the coffin, still desperate for money.
Comment: Describes a person who is really greedy.

guān cái
棺 材：coffin

lǐ
里：inside

guān cái lǐ
棺 材 里：in a coffin

shēn
伸：stick

chū
出：out, exit

shǒu
手：hand

lái
来：come

shēn chū shǒu lái
伸 出 手 来：the hand sticks out

sǐ
死：die

yào
要：want, ask for

sǐ yào
死 要：desparate

qián
钱：money

sǐ yào qián
死 要 钱：still desparate for money

比喻人爱财如命。

guì yì jiāo fù yì qī
贵 易 交, 富 易 妻。

Proverb: Once people become wealthy and achieve a higher social position; they will get rid of their old friends and original wife.
Comment: This does not describe a uniquely Chinese phenomenon. People who move up in life sometimes outgrow their old friends and take on a new "trophy wife."

guì fù guì
贵 = 富 贵：wealthy and achieve a higher social position

yì huàn
易 = 换：exchange, deal in, trade in

jiāo jiāo jì
交 = 交 际：social intercourse; means the people you socialize with

guì yì qī
贵 易 交：become wealthy and achieve a higher social position, then get rid of old friends, associate with new friends

fù fù guì
富 = 富 贵：wealthy and achieve a higher social position

qī
妻：wife

fù yì qī
富 易 妻：become wealthy and achieve a higher social position, then get rid of old wife, marry with a new and younger worman

易：改变，更换。指人的地位显贵了会抛弃旧时的患难之交，改结新贵；钱财富足了，会抛弃结发妻子另结新欢。

guò hé chāi qiáo xiè mò shā lǘ
过 河 拆 桥，卸 磨 杀 驴。

Proverb: Dismantle a bridge right after crossing the river; kill the donkey right after unloading the millstone.
Comment: Once you have no need for a person, drop him.

guò
过：cross

hé
河：a river

guò hé
过 河：cross a river

chāi
拆：dismantle

qiáo
桥：bridge

chāi qiáo
拆 桥：dismantle a bridge

guò hé chāi qiáo
过 河 拆 桥：dismantle a bridge right after crossing the river

xiè
卸：unload

mò
磨：millstone

shā
杀：kill

lǘ
驴：donkey

xiè mò shā lǘ
卸 磨 杀 驴：kill the donkey right after unloading the millstone

走过桥以后就认为再也用不上了，就把桥毁掉；驴拉完磨，就把它从磨杆上卸下来，杀掉。比喻利用完某人的价值以后，就一脚把他踢开，多用来指责忘恩负义的行为。

hǎo mǎ bù chī huí tóu cǎo
好 马 不 吃 回 头 草。

Proverb: A good horse will not turn back to eat the grass he just passed by.
Comment: Smart people stay focused. People also use this proverb as an excuse not to do something.

hǎo
好：good, fine

mǎ
马：horse

bù
不：no, not

chī
吃：eat

huí
回：go back

tóu
头：head

huí tóu
回 头：turn the head

cǎo
草：grass

huí tóu cǎo
回 头 草：the grass he just passed by

hǎo mǎ bù chī huí tóu cǎo
好 马 不 吃 回 头 草：a good horse will not turn back to eat the grass he just passed by

指聪明人做事拿定主意勇往直前，绝不中途反悔走回头路。

hǎo nán bù chī fēn jiā fàn hǎo nǚ bù chuān jià shí yī
好男不吃分家饭，好女不穿嫁时衣。

Proverb: A good son will not make a living by dividing up his family's property; a good daughter will not wear wedding clothes.
Comment: Ambitious people will not live off their parents' property.

hǎo
好：good, fine

nán
男：male, man

bù
不：no, not

chī
吃：eat

fēn jiā
分家：divide up family's property

fàn
饭：steamed rice

fēn jiā fàn
分家饭：live on the money by dividing up his family's property

nǚ
女：female, woman

hǎo nǚ
好女：a good woman

chuān
穿：wear

bù chuān
不穿：not wear

jià
嫁：marry

shí
时：time

yī
衣：clothes

jià shí yī
嫁时衣：wedding clothes

指有志气的男女不依靠婚嫁时父母所赠予的财产过活。

hǎo nán bù yú nǚ dòu hǎo gǒu bù yú jī dòu
好 男 不 与 女 斗，好 狗 不 与 鸡 斗。

Proverb: A good man will not fight a woman; a good dog will not fight a chicken.

Comment: This saying pretends to be the way of a gentleman, but it actually reflects the traditional Chinese attitude of looking down on women. Chickens and women here are lumped together.

hǎo
好：good, fine

nán
男：male, man

bù
不：no, not

yú hé
与 = 和：with

nǚ
女：female, woman

dòu
斗：fight

háo nán bù yú nǚ dòu
好 男 不 与 女 斗：a good man will not fight a woman

gǒu
狗：dog

hǎo gǒu
好 狗：a good dog

jī
鸡：chicken

dòu
斗：fight

hǎo gǒu bù yú jī dòu
好 狗 不 与 鸡 斗：a good dog will not fight a chicken

提倡绅士风度。旧时中国看不起女人，鸡和女人都属于弱势团体。

hé shàng kǒu chī biàn sì fāng xiù cái kǒu mà biàn sì fāng
和 尚 口 吃 遍 四 方，秀 才 口 骂 遍 四 方。

Proverb: A monk's mouth eats everywhere; a scholar's mouth talks with curses for everything.

Comment: Monks don't cook; they beg for food and take food wherever it's given. Scholars complain all the time.

hé shàng
和 尚：a monk

kǒu
口：mouth

chī
吃：eat

biàn
遍：all over

sì
四：four

fāng fāng xiàng
方 = 方 向：direction

sì fāng
四 方：4 directions: east, west, north & south; here means everywhere

hé shàng kǒu chī biàn sì fāng
和 尚 口 吃 遍 四 方：monk's mouth eats everywhere

xiù cái
秀 才：a scholar, a man who passed the imperial examination at the county level in the Ming and Qing dynasties

xiù cái kǒu
秀 才 口：a scholar's mouth

mà
骂：talk with curses; here means complain

mà biàn
骂 遍：talks with curses for everything

xiù cái kǒu mà biàn sì fāng
秀 才 口 骂 遍 四 方：a scholar's mouth talks with curses for everything

指和尚靠到处化斋来养活自己。读书人对什么都看不顺眼，满腹牢骚，因此什么都骂。

hé shàng niàn jīng　yǒu kǒu wú xīn
和　尚　念　经，有　口　无　心。

Proverb: A monk chants scripture with his mouth but not his heart.
Comment: Used to laugh at other people who do things without thinking.

hé shàng
和　尚：a monk

niàn
念：chant or read aloud

jīng　jīng wén
经 = 经　文：Buddhist religious scripture

hě shàng niàn jīn
和　尚　念 经：a monk chants scripture

yǒu
有：have

kǒu
口：mouth

yǒu kǒu
有　口：have a mouth

wú
无：without

xīn
心：heart; here means thinking

wú xīn
无　心：without thinking

yǒu kǒu wú xīn
有　口 无 心：chanting without thinking

指做事心不在焉。或是做事敷衍了事，不够专业。

hóu zi bù zuān quān duō shāi jǐ biàn luó
猴子不钻圈，多筛几遍锣。

Proverb: If the monkey will not go through the hoop, he should tap the gong several times.

Comment: This saying refers to animal street shows. If people won't fall into your trap, you have to make an extra effort.

hóu zi
猴子：monkey

bù
不：no, not; here means to refuse

zuān
钻：go through

quān
圈：a circle, a hoop

zuān quān
钻圈：jumping through a hoop; here means to fall into a trap

hóu zi bù zuān quān
猴子不钻圈：monkey refuse to go through a hoop

duō
多：many, much

shāi
筛：shiver, tap

duō shāi
多筛：tap more times

jǐ
几：several

biàn
遍：a number of times in doing somethings

jǐ biàn
几遍：several times

luó
锣：a gong

duō shāi jǐ biàn luó
多筛几遍锣：tap the gong several times

筛：敲。比喻对方不上圈套，就要多加引诱。

huàn	tāng	bú	huàn	yào
换	汤	不	换	药。

Proverb: Change the water but not the medicine.
Comment: In Chinese medicine, herbs are cooked in water. This saying means change only the name or format, not the substance.

huàn
换：change

tāng
汤：soup; here means water, use it for cooking medicinal herbs

bú
不：no, not

bú huàn
不 换：not change

yào
药：medicine; here means Chinese medicinal herbs

huàn tāng bú huàn yào
换 汤 不 换 药：change the water but not the herbs

熬药的水换了，但药没换。比喻只改了名称或形式，实质并没有改变。

画蛇添足
多此一举

huà shé tiān zú duō cǐ yī jǔ
画 蛇 添 足，多 此 一 举。

Proverb: Draw a snake, add a foot; one more unnecessary action.
Comment: The job is completed, but the worker does not stop.
Additional unnecessary work ruins the whole thing.

huà
画：draw, paint

shé
蛇：snake

tiān
添：add

zú
足：a foot

huà shé tiān zú
画 蛇 添 足：draw a snake, add a foot

duō
多：many, more

cǐ
此：this, these

yī
一：one

jǔ
举：raise; here also means an action

yī jǔ
一 举：one action

duō cǐ yī jǔ
多 此 一 举：one more unnecessary action

比喻已经做得圆满的事，还不收手，结果反而把事情搞坏了。

huà hǔ bù chéng fǎn lèi quǎn
画 虎 不 成 反 类 犬。

Proverb: Drew a tiger but it looks like a dog.

Comment: Some people try to accomplish something but they wind up falling short.

huà
画：draw

hǔ
虎：tiger

bù
不：no, not

chéng chéng góng
成 = 成 功：finish, succeed

huà hǔ bù chéng
画 虎 不 成：can't draw a tiger

fǎn fǎn ér
反 = 反 而：instead

lèi lèi shì
类 = 类 似：similar

quǎn gǒu
犬 = 狗：dog

fǎn lèi quǎn
反 类 犬：instead it looks like a dog

虎没画好，反倒画得像条狗。比喻别人的长处没学到，反而弄巧成拙。

huáng dì bù chāi è bīng
皇 帝 不 差 饿 兵。

Proverb: Even a king cannot give orders to starving soldiers.
Comment: The starving soldiers need to eat before they can fight.
Better pay in advance.

huáng dì
皇 帝：an emperor, a king

bù
不：no, not

chāi chāi qiǎn
差 = 差 遣：dispatch, order

è
饿：hungry, starve

bīng
兵：soldier

è bīng
饿 兵：starving soldier

huáng dì bù chāi è bīng
皇 帝 不 差 饿 兵：king cannot give orders to starving soldiers

即使是皇帝也不能让士兵饿着肚子去打仗，指差人干活首先得让人吃饱，也指差人做事得预先支付报酬。

huáng dì bù jí, jí sǐ tài jiān
皇帝不急，急死太监。

Proverb: The emperor is not in a hurry, but the eunuchs feel extremely hurried.
Comment: Eunuchs played a major role as assistants to the emperors in certain periods in Chinese history. The people in charge have less time pressure than those working for them do.

huáng dì
皇 帝：an emperor

bù
不：no, not

jí
急：hurry

huáng dì bù jí
皇 帝 不 急：the emperor is not in a hurry

sǐ
死：die; here means extremely

jí sǐ
急 死：extremely in a hurry

tài jiān
太 监：an eunuch

jí sǐ tài jiān
急 死 太 监：the eunuchs feel extremely hurried

比喻该着急的当事人不急，旁边不该着急的人却焦急万分。

huáng dì de nǚ er bù chóu jià
皇帝的女儿不愁嫁。

Proverb: An emperor's daughter need not worry about getting married.
Comment: Don't worry. Literally,a rich and powerful man's daughter will have no shortage of suiters. More generally, any good deal will be readily accepted.

huáng dì
皇帝：an emperor

dē
的：'s

nǚ er
女儿：daughter

huáng dì dē nǚ er
皇帝的女儿：an emperor's daughter

bù
不：no, not

chóu
愁：worry

jià
嫁：marry

bù chóu jià
不愁嫁：need not worry about getting married

皇帝的女儿不用发愁嫁不出去。比喻好的或者紧俏的商品不愁没有销路。

huáng dì fàng gè pì zhōu guān chàng tái xì
皇帝放个屁，州官唱台戏。

Proverb: The emperor releases gas; state officials make an entire performance on the stage.
Comment: People use this expressionproverb to laugh at others who exhibit sycophantic behavior.

huáng dì
皇帝：an emperor, king

fàng
放：release

gè
个：a unit word for count people

pì
屁：gas

fàng gè pì
放个屁：release a gas

zhōu
州：state

guān
官：goverment offical

zhōu guān
州官：an state goverment offical

chàng
唱：sing

tái
台：stage

xì
戏：performance

zhōu guān chàng tái xì
州官唱台戏：state officials make an entire performance on the stage

指上级随便说一句话或表个态，下属便急忙张罗，小题大做。讥讽官吏竭力巴结奉承上司。

huáng shǔ láng dān yǎo bìng yā zi
黄鼠狼单咬病鸭子。

Proverb: A weasel only bites a sick duck.

Comment: Disaster falls only on people who are poor and unfortunate.

huáng
黄：yellow

shǔ
鼠：mouse, rat

láng
狼：wolf

huáng shǔ láng
黄鼠狼：weasel

dān dān dān
单 = 单单：only

yǎo
咬：bite

bìng
病：ill, sick

yā zi
鸭子：duck

bìng yā zi
病鸭子：a sick duck

huáng shǔ láng dān yǎo bìng yā zi
黄鼠狼单咬病鸭子：weasel bites only a sick duck

比喻灾祸偏偏降临到不幸者的头上来。

huáng shǔ láng gěi jī bài nián méi ān hǎo xīn
黄 鼠 狼 给 鸡 拜 年—没 安 好 心。

Proverb: When a weasel says "Happy New Year" to the chicken, it's not with the best of intentions.
Comment: This is said to expose some people's two-facedness.

huáng
黄：yellow

shǔ
鼠：mouse, rat

láng
狼：wolf

huáng shǔ láng
黄 鼠 狼：weasel

gěi
给：give

jī
鸡：chicken

bài nián
拜 年：say "Happy New Year" on New Year's day

huáng shǔ láng gěi jī bài nián
黄 鼠 狼 给 鸡 拜 年：a weasel says "Happy New Year" to the chicken

méi méi yǒu
没 = 没 有：not have

ān
安：install

hǎo
好：good

xīn
心：heart

ān hǎo xīn
安 好 心：with the best of intentions

méi ān hǎo xīn
没 安 好 心：not with the best of intentions

黄鼠狼本来要吃鸡，却反过来给鸡拜年，显然是别有用心。指表面上献殷勤，心里却另打自己的主意。常用来揭露人伪装和伪善。

huì kū dē hái zi yǒu nǎi chī
会 哭 的 孩 子 有 奶 吃。

Proverb: The child who is good at crying gets the milk.
Comment: People who complain always gain more benefits than others. The squeaky wheel gets the grease is the American version.

huì
会：be good at

kū
哭：cry

dē
的：'s

hái zi
孩 子：child, children

huì kū dē hái zi
会 哭 的 孩 子：a child who is good at crying

yǒu
有：have

nǎi
奶：milk

chī
吃：eat; here means drink

yǒu nǎi chī
有 奶 吃：have milk to drink; here means gets the milk

比喻会抱怨的人，总能捞取到多一点的好处。

hún shuǐ lǐ hǎo mō yú
浑 水 里 好 摸 鱼。

Proverb: It's easy to catch a fish in muddy water.
Comment: Fish can't see so well in muddy water. Some people take advantage in troubled times.

hún
浑：muddy

shuǐ
水：water

hún shuǐ
浑 水：muddy water

lǐ
里：inside

hún shuǐ lǐ
浑 水 里：in muddy water

hǎo
好：good, fine; here means a good time, easy to do

mō
摸：touch by feeling

yú
鱼：fish

mō yú
摸 鱼：catch a fish

hún shuǐ lǐ hǎo mō yú
浑 水 里 好 摸 鱼：it's easy to catch a fish in muddy water

浑浊的水里容易捉到鱼。比喻乘混乱时机谋取利益。

huó rén bù néng ràng niào biē sǐ
活人不能让尿憋死。

Proverb: Living people can't kill themselves by refusing to urinate.
Comment: People should not allow themselves to be held back by petty rules.

rén
人：a person

huó rén
活 人：living people

bù
不：no, not

néng
能：can

bù néng
不 能：cannot

ràng
让：allow

niào
尿：urine

biē
憋：suppress, hold back

sǐ
死：die

biē sǐ
憋 死：kill himself by holding his breath or refusing to urinate

huó rén bù néng ràng niào biē sǐ
活 人 不 能 让 尿 憋 死：living people can't kill themselves by refusing to urinate

活人不能有尿不尿，让尿憋死。比喻不能被小事难住或被某些规定限制住，指处理事情要灵活，要多想办法为自己找出路。

jī bù zé shí hán bù zé yī huāng bù zé lù pín bù zé qī
饥不择食，寒不择衣，慌不择路，贫不择妻。

Proverb: A hungry person is not picky about food; a cold person is not picky about what to wear; a person who is nervous will not choose a route to escape; a poor person cannot be picky about choosing a wife.
Comment: Standards get lowered when circumstances require it.

jī = jī è
饥 = 饥饿：hungry

bù
不：no, not

zé = xuǎn zé
择 = 选择：choose

shí
食：food

jī bù zé shí
饥不择食：a hungry person is not picky about food

hán = hán lěng
寒 = 寒冷：cold

yī
衣：clothes

hán bù zé yī
寒不择衣：a cold person is not picky about what to wear

huāng = huāng luàn
慌 = 慌乱：nervous

lù
路：way

huāng bù zé lù
慌不择路：a person who is nervous will not choose a route to escape

pín = pín qióng
贫 = 贫穷：poor

qī
妻：wife

pín bù zé qī
贫不择妻：a poor person cannot be picky about choosing a wife

饥饿的时候，能有充饥的食物就好。寒冷的时候，能有御寒的衣服就行。惊慌赶路时，来不及选择道路。贫穷时，有人嫁给他就不错了。比喻条件不好时要求不能太高，只能退而求次了。

jī dàn lǐ tiāo gú tou
鸡 蛋 里 挑 骨 头。

Proverb: Pick a bone from an egg.
Comment: Eggs don’t have bones. This means finding a problem where none exists.

jī
鸡：chicken

dàn
蛋：an egg

jī dàn
鸡 蛋：chicken’s egg

lǐ lǐ miàn
里 = 里 面：inside, within

jī dàn lǐ
鸡 蛋 里：from chicken’s egg

tiāo
挑：pick

gú tou
骨 头：a bone

tiāo gú tou
挑 骨 头：pick a bone

jī dàn lǐ tiāo gú tou
鸡 蛋 里 挑 骨 头：pick a bone from an egg

在鸡蛋里寻找骨头。比喻故意挑毛病，多用来指责人过分挑剔。

jī wō lǐ fēi chū gē jīn fèng huáng
鸡 窝 里 飞 出 个 金 凤 凰。

Proverb: A golden phoenix flies out from a chicken's nest.
Comment: Arduous conditions or adverse circumstances still can foster good and talented people.

jī
鸡：chicken

wō
窝：nest

lǐ　　lǐ miàn
里 = 里 面：inside

jī wō lǐ
鸡 窝 里：in the chicken's nest

fēi
飞：fly

chū
出：exit, come out

gē
个：a measure word for phoenix

jīn
金：gold

fèng huáng
凤　凰：phoenix, a legendary bird from Chinese traditions

jīn fèng huáng
金 凤　凰：golden phoenix

jī wō lǐ fēi chū gē jīn fèng huáng
鸡 窝 里 飞 出 个 金 凤　凰：a golden phoenix flies out from a chicken's nest

比喻条件艰苦或环境恶劣的地方也能出人材。

jiā huā nǎ yǒu yě huā xiāng
家 花 哪 有 野 花 香。

Proverb: How can a home flower smell better than a wild flower?
Comment: Used to laugh at men who have love affairs, pursue the new, and dump the old.

jiā
家：home, family

huā
花：flower; here means women

jiā huā
家 花：home flower; here means wife

nǎ nǎ lǐ
哪 = 哪 里：where

yǒu
有：have

yě
野：wild

yě huā
野 花：wild flower; here means a woman outside of the family

xiāng
香：fragrant, sweet-smelling

jiā huā nǎ yǒu yě huā xiāng
家 花 哪 有 野 花 香：how can a home flower smell better then a wild flower

家花：比喻妻、妾。野花：比喻妓女或外遇的女人。妻妾不如外遇的女人好。多用来讥讽男子拈花惹草，喜新厌旧。

jiā jiā yǒu běn nán niàn dē jīng
家 家 有 本 难 念 的 经。

Proverb: Every family has a difficult scripture to chant.
Comment: Every family has to deal with its own problems.

jiā
家：home, family

jiā jiā
家 家：every family

yǒu
有：have

běn
本：a measure word of scripture

nán
难：difficult

niàn
念：chant

dē
的：'s

nán niàn dē
难 念 的：difficult to chant

jīng
经：Buddhist scripture

jiā jiā yǒu běn bán niàn dē jīng
家家有本 难 念 的经：every family has a difficult scripture to chant

念经：念佛教的经典，难念的经是指难以解决的事。指家家都有难办的事。

jià chū qù dē nǚ er pō chū qù dē shuǐ
嫁 出 去 的 女 儿 泼 出 去 的 水。

Proverb: A daughter gets married off, just like water is poured out.
Comment: In traditional China, parents did not want to spend money on a daughter's education because the daughter, when married, would join another family.

jià
嫁：marry

chū qù
出 去：get out, exit

dē
的：'s

nǚ er
女 儿：daughter

jià chū qù dē nǚ er
嫁 出 去 的 女 儿：a daughter married off

pō
泼：pour, splash

pō chū qù dē
泼 出 去 的：pour out

shuǐ
水：water

pō chū qù dē shuǐ
泼 出 去 的 水：water is poured out

嫁女儿就像泼水一样，不再是娘家的人，娘家父母也管不了。旧时重男轻女，因此常表现在幼年养育时也不愿多花钱让她们接受教育。

jià hàn jià hàn chuān yī chī fàn
嫁汉嫁汉，穿衣吃饭。

Proverb: Marry a man for clothes and food.

Comment: This is a traditional view of marriage.

jià
嫁：marry

hàn
汉：a Chinese man

jià hàn
嫁 汉：marry a man

jià hàn jià hàn
嫁 汉 嫁 汉：marry a man, marry a man

chuān
穿：wear

yī
衣：clothes

chī
吃：eat

fàn
饭：boiled or teamed rice

chī fàn
吃 饭：eat meals

jià hàn jià hàn chuān yī chī fàn
嫁 汉 嫁 汉，穿 衣 吃 饭：marry a man, marry a man, for clothes and food

指旧时的女人嫁人，主要是为了找个人来养活她自己。

jià jī suí jī jià gǒu suí gǒu jià lē hóu zi mǎn shān zǒu
嫁鸡随鸡，嫁狗随狗，嫁了猴子满山走。

Proverb: If a woman marries a chicken, she has to follow the chicken; if she marries a dog, she must follow the dog; if she marries a monkey, she has to walk with the monkey all over the mountains.
Comment: A woman should marry only once and be with her husband all her life. The man, in the Confucian system, is the center of the family.

jià
嫁：marry

jī
鸡：chicken

suí gēn suí
随 = 跟 随：follow

jià jī suí jī
嫁鸡随鸡：marries a chicken, follow the chicken

gǒu
狗：dog

jià gǒu suí gǒu
嫁狗随狗：marries a dog, follow the dog

lē
了：no meaning, use after a verb to show change already finished

jià lē
嫁了：married

hóu zi
猴子：monkey

mǎn
满：full

shān
山：mountain

mǎn shān
满山：all over the mountain

zǒu
走：walk

jià lē hóu zi mǎn shān zǒu
嫁了猴子满山走：marries a monkey, she has to walk with the monkey all over the mountains

旧时提倡女子从一而终，不管嫁的是什么人，都要跟他过一辈子。

jiāng hái shì lǎo dē là
姜 还 是 老 的 辣。

Proverb: Nevertheless, the old ginger is hotter.

Comment: Old people have more experience and wisdom.

jiāng
姜：ginger

hái shì
还 是：nevertheless

lǎo
老：old

dē
的：'s

là
辣：hot

lǎo dē là
老 的 辣：old is hotter

jiāng hái shì lǎo dē là
姜 还 是 老 的 辣：nevertheless, the old ginger is hotter

"姜还是老的辣"通常是在事情过后给人好印象、好评价时说的。即是说人成熟了，经验也丰富了。

jiāng tài gōng diào yú yuàn zhě shàng gōu
姜 太 公 钓 鱼，愿 者 上 钩。

Proverb: Mr. Jiang is fishing; any fish who is willing can bite the hook.
Comment: Jiang Taigong was a real person in the eleventh century BC. Jiang fished with a with a bamboo pole that had a barbless hook attached to it. He believed the fish would come to him of their own volition when they were ready. People use this proverb to tell others that something is not a trap. Nobody forces you to do something, so stop complaining.

jiāng tài gōng
姜 太 公：Mr. Jiang

diào
钓：fishing

yú
鱼：a fish

jiāng tài gōng diào yú
姜 太 公 钓 鱼：Mr. Jiang is fishing

yuàn yuàn yì
愿 = 愿 意：be willing

zhě
者：people, a person

yuàn zhě
愿 者：anyone who is willing

gōu
钩：a hook

shàng gōu
上 钩：bite a hook

yuàn zhě shàng gōu
愿 者 上 钩：anyone who is willing can bite a hook

姜太公还是贫民时用直钩钓鱼，而且不挂鱼饵，照样也有鱼上钩。
比喻没人逼着你去干某一件事，是你自己心甘情愿地上圈套，因此没有什么好埋怨的。

jiāo huì tú dì è sǐ shī fù
教 会 徒 弟，饿 死 师 傅。

Proverb: The master teaches the apprentice to learn the task, and the master starves to death.

Comment: Train your apprentice, and you create a competitor.

jiāo
教：teach

huì xué huì
会 = 学 会：learned

jiāo huì
教 会：learned the task

tú dì
徒弟：an apprentice

jiāo huì tú dì
教 会 徒 弟：teaches the apprentice to learn the task

è
饿：starve

sǐ
死：death

è sǐ
饿 死：starve to death

shī fù
师 傅：master

è sǐ shī fù
饿 死 师 傅：master starves to death

比喻帮助人也不能帮得太多，增加别人的竞争力只会让自己倒霉。

jìn shuǐ lóu tái xiān dé yuè xiàng yáng huā mù yì wéi chūn
近水楼台先得月，向阳花木易为春。

Proverb: The moon reflects first on the building with a terrace near the water; spring comes earlier to flowers and trees that face the sun.
Comment: If you have a connection, you get a benefit first.

jìn
近：near

shuǐ
水：water

lóu
楼：building

tái
台：terrace

xiān
先：first

dé
得：get

yuè
月：moon

jìn shuǐ lóu tái xiān dé yuè
近水楼台先得月：the moon reflects first on the building with a terrace near the water

xiàng
向：face

yáng
阳：sun

xiàng yáng
向阳：face the sun

huā
花：flower

mù
木：wood

huā mù
花木：flowers and trees

yì róng yì
易 = 容易：easy

wéi
为：become

chūn
春：spring

xiàng yáng huā mù yì wéi chūn
向阳花木易为春：spring comes earlier to flowers and trees that face the sun

水边的楼台没有树木的遮挡，能先看到月亮的投影；而迎着阳光的花木，光照好，所以发芽就早，最容易形成春天的景象。指因为近便先得到好处，也指某些人靠关系办事而得益。

jìng jiǔ bù chī chī fá jiǔ
敬 酒 不 吃 吃 罚 酒。

Proverb: Refuse a toast, and you will be forced to drink as punishment.
Comment: This saying is used to threaten people who don't respond to polite requests. They will suffer hardships and be forced to comply anyway.

jìng gōng jìng
敬 = 恭 敬：respectful

jiǔ
酒：wine

jìng jiǔ
敬 酒：drink with great respect, propose a toast

bù
不：no, not

chī
吃：eat; here means drink

bù chī
不 吃：not drink

jiù jìng bù chī
敬 酒 不 吃：refuse a toast

fá
罚：punish

fá jiǔ
罚 酒：a penal drink

hē fá jiǔ
吃 罚 酒：be forced to drink as punishment

jiù jǐng bù chī chī fá jiǔ
敬 酒 不 吃 吃 罚 酒：refuse a toast, then you will be forced to drink as punishment

敬酒就是用恭敬的态度请人喝酒，罚酒就是用强硬的态度罚人喝酒。比喻好言相劝不听，非让人强迫才行。多用来威胁人不听劝告，将要吃苦头，受责罚。

jìng le fù mǔ bú pà tiān nà le juān shuì bú pà guān
敬了父母不怕天，纳了捐 税不怕 官。

Proverb: If you show filial piety and respect for your parents, you have no need to be afraid of God's punishment; if you pay your taxes, you have no need to be afraid of the government officials.
Comment: Do your duty, obey the law and you will have nothing to fear.

jìng xiào jìng
敬 = 孝 敬：show filial piety and respect for parents

lē
了：no meaning, used after a verb to show change already finished

fù mǔ
父母：parent

bú
不：no, not

pà
怕：afraid

tiān
天：sky, means god

bú pà tiān
不怕天：not afraid God's punishment

jìng lē fù mǔ bú pà tiān
敬了父母不怕天：if you show filial piety and respect for your parents, you have no need to be afraid of God's punishment

nà jiāo nà
纳 = 交 纳：pay

juān shuì
捐 税：tax

guān
官：goverment official

nà lē juān shuì bú pà guān
纳了捐 税 不 怕 官：if you pay your taxes, no need to be afraid of the government officials

做到了孝敬父母，就不怕老天爷惩罚；交纳了税款就不用怕官府找麻烦。
指做事走正道，就什么都不怕。

jiǔ bìng chuáng qián wú xiào zǐ
久 病 床 前 无 孝 子。

Proverb: If a parent is sick too long, no dutiful children will be waiting in front of the bed.

Comment: If people are sick for a long time, even their own kids will lose patience.

jiǔ
久：for a long time

bìng
病：ill, sick

jiǔ bìng
久 病：sick for a long time

chuáng
床：bed

qián
前：in front of

chuáng qián
床 前：in front of the bed

wú méi yǒu
无 = 没 有：not have

xiào zǐ
孝 子：dutiful children

jiǔ bìng chuáng qián wú xiào zǐ
久病 床 前无 孝子：if a parent is sick too long, no dutiful children will be waiting in front of the bed

指卧病时间长了，亲生儿女也会产生厌烦情绪，不再耐心伺候。

jiǔ	hòu	tǔ	zhēn	yán
酒	后	吐	真	言。

Proverb: After drinking some wine, you will tell the truth.

Comment: Alcohol loosens the tongue.

jiǔ
酒：wine

hòu
后：after

jiǔ hòu
酒 后：after drinking wine

tǔ　　tǔ lù
吐 = 吐 露：tell

zhēn
真：truth

yán
言：speech or word

zhēn yán
真 言：tell the truth

jiǔ hòu tǔ zhēn yán
酒 后 吐 真 言：after drinking some wine, you will tell the truth

喝醉酒以后控制不住自己，讲的都是平时不讲的真话。

jiǔ shì chuān cháng dú yào sè shì guā gǔ gāng dāo
酒 是 穿 肠 毒 药, 色 是 刮 骨 钢 刀。

Proverb: Wine is poison that passes through your gut; lust is like a knife that scrapes your bones.

Comment: Too much alchohol and too much sex can be bad for health..

jiǔ
酒：wine

shì
是：is, are

chuān
穿：pass through

cháng
肠：gut

chuān cháng
穿 肠：pass through the gut

dú
毒：poison

yào
药：medicine

jiǔ shì chuān chuáng dú yào
酒是 穿 肠 毒 药：wine is poison that passes through your gut

sè
色：lust

guā
刮：scrape

gǔ
骨：bone

gāng
钢：stell

dāo
刀：knife

sè shì guā gǔ gāng dāo
色 是 刮 骨 钢 刀：lust is like a knife that scrapes your bones

指好酒和好色都会损害人的健康。

jiù jí bú jiù qióng
救 急 不 救 穷。

Proverb: Help in emergencies; do not help the poor.

Comment: Chinese believe that one should help in emergencies.
But helping the poor will create a dependency and a burden.

jiù
救：rescue, help

jí
急：emergency

jiù jí
救急：help in emergencies

bú
不：no, not

bú jiù
不救：not help

qióng
穷：poor

jiù qióng
救穷：help poor

jiù jí bú jiù qióng
救急不救穷：help in emergencies, do not help the poor

救人于急难之中，哪怕千金也不吝惜；但单纯地给予穷人钱财，最终只会将自己拖累。

kǒu huì ér shí bù zhì
口 惠 而 实 不 至。

Proverb: Promises are words, but not deeds.

Comment: "Actions speak louder than words" might be the American equivalent.

kǒu zuǐ
口 = 嘴：mouth

huì
惠：favor

kǒu huì
口 惠：promises a favor in words

ér
而：a link word between two things; here means but

shí shí jì
实 = 实 际：in fact

bù
不：no, not

zhì
至：come

shí bù zhì
实 不 至：in fact things not come

kǒu huì ér shí bù zhì
口 惠 而 实 不 至：promises are words, but not deeds

惠：给人以好处。口惠：口头上许诺的好处。指只是在口头上答应给人好处，却不见实际利益的落实。

kuài dāo qiē dòu fu liǎng miàn guāng
快刀切豆腐，两面光。

Proverb: A sharp knife slices the bean curd; both sides are smooth.

Comment: This proverb is said about a person who does not take sides and pleases everybody in solving a problem.

kuài
快：fast; here means sharp

dāo
刀：a knife

kuài dāo
快 刀：a sharp knife

qiē
切：cut, slice

dòu fu
豆 腐：bean curd

kuài dāo qiē dòu fu
快 刀 切 豆 腐：a sharp knife slices the bean curd

liǎng
两：two

miàn
面：side

liǎng miàn
两 面：both sides

guāng
光：bright; here means smooth

liǎng miàn guāng
两 面 光：both sides are smooth

指问题迎刃而解，办得干脆利索；两面光，两不沾。比喻两面讨好。

kuài zi tóu shàng chū nì zi bàng zi dǐ xià chū xiào zi
筷子头上出逆子，棒子底下出孝子。

Proverb: With chopsticks, raise a disobedient son; with a stick, raise a dutiful son.
Comment: Equivalent to "spare the rod, spoil the child."

kuài zi
筷子：chopsticks

tóu
头：head

shàng
上：on top of

kuài zi tóu shàng
筷子头上：on the top of chopsticks; here means feed to much, spoil the children

chū
出：exit, produce

nì wǔ nì
逆 = 忤逆：disobedient

zi hái zi
子 = 孩子：children

chū nì zi
出逆子：raise a disobedient child

bàng zi
棒子：stick

dǐ
底：bottom

xià
下：below, under

bàng zi dǐ xià
棒子底下：under the stick; here means physical punishment

xiào xiào shùn
孝 = 孝顺：show filial obedience and devotion for his parents

xiào zi
孝子：a dutiful son

chū xiào zi
出孝子：raise a dutiful son

指从小严加管教，长大后才会孝顺父母，娇生惯养就会出逆子。

lài	há	má	xiǎng	chī	tiān	é	ròu
癞	蛤	蟆	想	吃	天	鹅	肉。

Proverb: A toad wants to eat swan meat.

Comment: A toad is ugly; a swan is beautiful. Used to describe a woman and man's relationship in which the man is poor and ugly and below the level of the woman.

lài há má
癞 蛤 蟆：a toad; here means a poor or ugly man

xiǎng
想：think, wish

chī
吃：eat

xiǎng chī
想 吃：want to eat

tiān é
天 鹅：swan; here means a beautiful woman

ròu
肉：meat

lài há má xiǎng chī tiān é ròu
癞 蛤 蟆 想 吃 天 鹅 肉：a toad wants to eat swan meat

地上爬着的癞哈蟆，想吃天上飞的天鹅肉。比喻想得太美，根本达不到目的。是讥笑人的话，多用于男女关系。

lǎn lǘ zi shàng mò shǐ niào duō
懒 驴 子 上 磨 屎 尿 多。

Proverb: Once a lazy donkey starts working at the mill, he will have more excrement and urine than usual.
Comment: This is an insult used against lazy people.

lǎn
懒：lazy

lǘ zi
驴 子：a donkey

shàng
上：get on

mò
磨：a mill

shàng mò
上 磨：start work at the mill

lǎn lǘ zi shàng mò
懒 驴 子 上 磨：a lazy donkey starts working at the mill

shǐ
屎：excrement

niào
尿：urine

duō
多：more, much

lǎn lǘ zi shàng mò shǐ niào duō
懒 驴 子 上 磨 屎 尿 多：once a lazy donkey starts working at the mill, he will have more excrement and urine then usual

常用来骂人的话，指懒人一到干活的时候就磨蹭偷懒，消磨时间。

lǎn pó niáng dē guǒ jiǎo bù yòu chòu yòu cháng
懒 婆 娘 的 裹 脚 布，又 臭 又 长。

Proverb: The cotton cloth binding a lazy woman's feet is too stinky and too long.

Comment: Historically, women's feet were bound to make small feet in China. This proverb is used to criticize someone's speech or article.

lǎn
懒：lazy

pó niáng
婆 娘：woman

dē
的：'s

guǒ
裹：wind around

jiǎo
脚：feet

bù
布：cotton cloth

guǒ jiǎo bù
裹 脚 布：a long narrow cotton cloth, used to bind feet

lǎn pó niáng dē guǒ jiǎo bù
懒 婆 娘 的 裹 脚 布：the cotton cloth binding a lazy woman's feet

yòu
又：both

chòu
臭：stinky

cháng
长：long

yòu chòu yòu cháng
又 臭 又 长：both too stinky and too long

裹脚布：缠小脚用的布。形容文章或讲话的篇幅太长，内容却非常糟糕。

lǎo hǔ pì gǔ mō bù dé
老虎屁股摸不得。

Proverb: Cannot touch a tiger's bottom.

Comment: Some people are too proud or too sensitive and cannot take criticism.

lǎo hǔ
老虎：tiger

pì gǔ
屁股：bottom

lǎo hǔ pì gǔ
老虎屁股：a tiger's bottom

mō
摸：feel by touch

bù dé
不得：cannot, not be allowed

mō bù dé
摸不得：cannot touch

lǎo hǔ pì gǔ mō bù dé
老虎屁股摸不得：cannot touch a tiger's bottom

比喻某些人骄傲自满，或专横跋扈，别人批评冒犯不得。

lǎo	hǔ	tóu	shàng	pāi	cāng	yíng
老	虎	头	上	拍	苍	蝇。

Proverb: Swat a fly on a tiger's head.

Comment: You cannot offend evil people unless you want to die.

lǎo hǔ
老 虎：tiger

tóu
头：head

shàng
上：above, on the top of

tóu shàng
头 上：on the head

pāi
拍：swat

cāng yíng
苍 蝇：a fly

lǎo hǔ tóu shàng pāi cāng yíng
老虎头上拍苍蝇：swat a fly on a tiger's head

指冒犯凶恶的人，等于自取灭亡。

lǎo shǔ diào jìn mǐ gāng lǐ
老 鼠 掉 进 米 缸 里。

Proverb: A mouse drops into a rice vat.

Comment: This saying signifies a big opportunity. Being dropped into a rice vat is a big bonanza for a mouse.

lǎo shǔ
老 鼠：mouse

diào
掉：drop

jìn
进：into

diào jìn
掉 进：drop into

mǐ
米：rice

gāng
缸：a vat, a jar

mǐ gāng
米 缸：rice vat

lǐ
里：inside, within

mǐ gāng lǐ
米 缸 里：in the rice vat

lǎo shǔ diào jìn mǐ gāng lǐ
老 鼠 掉 进 米 缸 里：a mouse drops in to a rice vat

指运气好，老鼠本身爱大米，现在得到一个能满足欲望的极好机会。

lǎo wáng mài guā zì mài zì kuā
老 王 卖 瓜，自 卖 自 夸。

Proverb: Old Mr. Wang sells melons; he brags that his melons are the best.

Comment: This is said to laugh at people who brag that their things are the best.

lǎo
老：old

wáng
王：Wang, it's a family name

lǎo wáng
老 王：an old man Mr. Wang

mài
卖：sell

guā
瓜：melon

lǎo wáng mài guā
老 王 卖 瓜：an old Mr. Wang sells melons

zì
自：self

zì mài
自 卖：he sells

kuā
夸：brag

zì kuā
自 夸：he brags

zì mài zì kuā
自 卖 自 夸：he brags his melons are the best

指自己夸耀自己的东西好或是自己夸自己好。

lǎo zi tōu guā dào guǒ ér zi shā rén fàng huǒ
老子偷瓜盗果，儿子杀人放火。

Proverb: If a father steals melons and fruit, his son will kill people and set fires.
Comment: Parents' bad examples will negatively influence their children.

lǎo zi
老子：one's father, an old man

tōu tōu qiè
偷 = 偷窃：steal

guā
瓜：melon

dào dào qiè
盗 = 盗窃：steal

guǒ
果：fruit

lǎo zi tōu guā dào guǒ
老子偷瓜盗果：a father steals melons and fruit

ér zi
儿子：son

shā
杀：kill

rén
人：people, a person

fàng
放：set

huǒ
火：fire

ér zi shā rén fàng huǒ
儿子杀人放火：son will kill people and set fires

父母如果榜样没做好，就会影响子女犯更大的错误。

lǐ xià yú rén bì yǒu suǒ qiú
礼 下 于 人，必 有 所 求。

Proverb: If someone is overly polite, he must have a request.
Comment: Beware when people are too polite.

lǐ lǐ yù
礼 = 礼 遇：courteous treatment; here means overly polite

xià
下：blew, under, down

yú gěi
于 = 给：give

rén
人：people, a person

lǐ xià yú rén
礼 下 于 人：overly polite to people

bì bì dìng
必 = 必 定：must be

yǒu
有：have, has

suǒ
所：therefor

qiú
求：request

bì yǒu suǒ qiú
必 有 所 求：must have his request

礼：礼遇。下于：给予。待人过分客气，必有企图。

guā tián bú nà lǚ lǐ xià bù zhěng guān
瓜田不纳履，李下不整冠。

Proverb: Don't adjust your shoes when walking in a melon patch; don't rearrange your hat when walking under a palm tree.
Comment: Doing these things from far away looks like you are stealing something. Be careful not to make people suspicious.

guā
瓜：melon

tián
田：farmland; for melons, a melon patch

bú
不：no, not

nà lǚ tí xié
纳履 = 提鞋：adjust the shoe

guā tián bú nà lǚ
瓜田不纳履：don't adjust your shoes when walking in a melon patch

lǐ lǐ shù
李 = 李树：plum tree

xià
下：below, under

lǐ xià
李下：under the plum tree

zhěng zhěng lǐ
整 = 整理：arrange

guān mào zǐ
冠 = 帽子：hat

zhěng guān
整冠：rearrange the hat

lǐ xià bù zhěng guān
李下不整冠：don't rearrange your hat when walking under a palm tree

在瓜地里不弯腰提鞋，避免让人怀疑在偷摘瓜。在李树下不举手整理帽子，避免让人怀疑在偷摘李子。比喻做事小心谨慎，避免引起不必要的误会。

liǎn	chǒu	guài	jìng	zǐ
脸	丑	怪	镜	子。

Proverb: Blame the mirror if your face is ugly.

Comment: If you have a defect or mistake, don't push the responsibility on other people.

liǎn
脸：face

chǒu nǎn kàn
丑 = 难 看：ugly

liǎn chǒu
脸 丑：an ugly-looking face

guài zé guài
怪 = 责 怪：blame

jìng zǐ
镜 子：a mirror

liǎn chǒu guài jìng zǐ
脸 丑 怪 镜 子：blame the mirror if your face is ugly

自己的脸长得不好看，不能责怪镜子照得不真。指自身有缺点，不能把责任推给别人

liǎn shàng dài xiào xiù lǐ cáng dāo
脸 上 带 笑，袖 里 藏 刀。

Proverb: Smile on the face, but a knife hidden in the sleeve.

Comment: In ancient times Chinese men's clothes had a pocket in the sleeves. This refers to somebody who looks very polite and friendly but is vicious at heart.

liǎn
脸：face

shàng
上：on the top of

liǎn shàng
脸 上：on the face

dài
带：carry

xiào
笑：a smile

liǎn shàng dài xiào
脸 上 带 笑：smile on the face

xiù yī xiù
袖 = 衣 袖：a sleeve

lǐ lǐ miàn
里 = 里 面：inside

xiù lǐ
袖 里：in the sleeve

cáng
藏：hide, store

dāo
刀：a knife

cáng dāo
藏 刀：hide a knife

xiù lǐ cáng dāo
袖 里 藏 刀：a knife hidden in the sleeve

脸上虽然笑着，袖子里却藏着尖刀，随时可以伤害人。形容表面客气，内心狠毒。

lóng jū qiǎn shuǐ zāo xiā xì hǔ luò píng yáng bèi quǎn qī

龙居浅水遭虾戏，虎落平阳被犬欺。

Proverb: If a dragon is living in the shallow water, it will be made a fool of by the shrimp; if a tiger meets with misfortune and comes to a plain and bright place, it will be humiliated by a dog.

Comment: Once you lose power, you will be humiliated by people who were below you.

lóng
龙：dragon

jū jū zhù
居 = 居住：live

qiǎn
浅：shallow

shuǐ
水：water

zāo
遭：meet with

xiā
虾：shrimp

xì xì lòng
戏 = 戏弄：make a fool of

lóng jū qiǎn shuǐ zāo xiā xì
龙居浅水遭虾戏：if dragon is living in the shallow water, it will be made a fool by the shrip

hǔ
虎：tiger

luò luò nàn
落 = 落难：meet with misfortune

píng yáng
平阳：a plain and bright place

bèi
被：by

quǎn
犬：dog

qī qī fù
欺 = 欺负：humiliate

hǔ luò píng yáng bèi quǎn qī
虎落平阳被犬欺：if a tiger meets with misfortune and comes to a plain and bright place, it will be humiliated by a dog

平阳：地势平坦明亮的地方。龙一到浅水中，虾也会戏弄它。老虎离开深山，落到平地里受困。比喻失势。指人在失去权势以后，反受到下等人的欺负。

lóng pà jiē lín hǔ pà chōu jīn
龙 怕 揭 鳞，虎 怕 抽 筋。

Proverb: A dragon is afraid of having its scales peeled off; a tiger is afraid of having its veins ripped out.
Comment: People all fear damage to their vital parts.

lóng
龙：dragon

pà
怕：afraid, fear

jiē
揭：peel off

lín
鳞：scale

jiē lín
揭 鳞：peel off the scales

lóng pà jiē lín
龙 怕 揭 鳞：a dragon is afraid having its scales peeled off

hǔ
虎：tiger

chōu
抽：rip out

jīn
筋：vein

chōu jīn
抽 筋：ripped the vein out

hǔ pà chōu jīn
虎 怕 抽 筋：a tiger is afraid of having its veins ripped out

比喻人都是怕伤到要害处的。

lóng shēng lóng fèng shēng fèng lǎo shǔ shēng ér dǎ dì dòng
龙 生 龙，凤 生 凤，老 鼠 生 儿 打 地 洞。

Proverb: A dragon gives birth to a dragon; a phoenix gives birth to a phoenix; a mouse's son can only dig a hole in the ground.
Comment: People's behavior is determined by their ancestry.

lóng
龙：dragon

shēng
生：give birth to

lóng shēng lóng
龙 生 龙：a dragon gives birth to a dragon

fèng
凤：phoenix

fèng shēng fèng
凤 生 凤：a phoenix gives birth to a phoenix

lǎo shǔ
老 鼠：mouse

ér ér zǐ
儿 = 儿 子：son

shēng ér
生 儿：give birth to a son

lǎo shǔ shēng ér
老 鼠 生 儿：a mouse gives birth to a son

dǎ
打：dig

dì
地：earth, ground

dòng
洞：a hole

dǎ dì dòng
打 地 洞：dig a hole in the ground

血统论，指基因将影响后代。

má què suī xiǎo wǔ zàng jù quán
麻雀虽小，五脏俱全。

Proverb: A sparrow, though small, still has all five internal organs.
Comment: Even a small-scale organization still can provide all kinds of indispensable functions.

má què
麻雀：sparrow

suī suī rán
虽 = 虽然：though

xiǎo
小：little, small

má què suī xiǎo
麻雀虽小：a sparrow, though small

wǔ zàng
五脏：five internal organs: heart, liver, spleen, lungs and kidneys

jù quán
具全：have them all

wǔ zàng jù quán
五脏具全：has all five internal organs

指即使是规模很小的机构，也都有各种必备的功能。

mǎ xíng wú lì jiē yīn shòu rén bù fēng liú zhǐ wéi pín
马 行 无力皆因 瘦，人 不风 流只为 贫。

Proverb: A horse walks without strength because it is thin; a man has no women only because he has no money.
Comment: No money no honey.

mǎ
马：horse

xíng xíng zǒu
行 = 行 走：walk

wú
无：without

lì
力：strength

jiē dū shì
皆 = 都是：all

yīn yīn wèi
因 = 因 为：because

shòu
瘦：thin

mǎ xíng wú lì jiē yīn shòu
马 行 无力皆因 瘦：a horse walks without strength all because it is thin

rén
人：a person

bù
不：not

fēng liú
风 流：dissolute

rén bù fēng liú
人 不 风 流：a man is not dissolute

zhǐ
只：just

wéi yīn wèi
为 = 因 为：because

pín
贫：poor, no money

zhǐ wéi pín
只 为 贫：just because he has no money

皆：都，都是。风流：好的一面指有风度而不拘礼法，坏的一面指男女之间放荡的行为。马走不动路是因为太瘦弱，人不风流也不是不想风流，而是因为家境贫穷手中缺钱，没有条件去风流。人的经济地位决定人的行为风范。

mǎi dé qǐ mǎ pèi bù qǐ ān
买得起马，配不起鞍。

Proverb: Can afford to buy a horse, cannot afford to buy a saddle.
Comment: Used to sneer at stingy people. If you spend big money, why not spend small money to make things perfect?

mǎi
买：buy

mǎ
马：horse

mǎi dé qǐ
买得起：can afford

mǎi bù qǐ
买不起：can not afford

mǎi dé qǐ mǎ
买得起马：can aford to buy a horse

pèi
配：match

pèi bù qǐ
配不起：cannot aford to buy

ān
鞍：saddle

pèi bù qǐ ān
配不起鞍：cannot afford to buy a saddle

用来嘲笑人吝啬，既然大钱也花了，为什么不肯再花一些必须花的小钱。

mǎi yī fú kàn xiù zi tǎo lǎo pó kàn jiù zi
买衣服看袖子，讨老婆看舅子。

Proverb: When buying clothes, pay attention to the sleeves; when taking a wife, look at the woman's brother.
Comment: In traditional times, a man had little opportunity to meet with his future wife. So he was well advised to check out her brother to get some idea about her looks and character.

mǎi
买：buy

yī fú
衣服：clothes

kàn
看：look, check, pay attention

xiù zi
袖子：sleeve

kàn xiù zi
看袖子：look at sleeve; here means see the stitch's quality

mǎi yī fú kàn xiù zi
买衣服看袖子：buy clothing should pay attention to the sleeves

tǎo
讨：take

lǎo pó
老婆：wife

jiù zi
舅子：wife's brother

kàn jiù zi
看舅子：look at wife's brother; means guess what she is by her brother

tǎo lǎo pó kàn jiù zi
讨老婆看舅子：take a wife should look at her brother

看了衣袖，就知道整件衣裳的质地和做功。看了舅子就能推测妻子的品貌和才能；也比喻通过对相关部分的观察，就可以推测出整个事物的全貌。

mǎn kǒu rén yì dào dé yī dù zi nán dào nǚ chāng
满口仁义道德，一肚子男盗女娼。

Proverb: He always talks about virtue and morality but always thinks about the dirty things, as do ruffians and whores.
Comment: This saying refers to people who are two-faced.

mǎn
满：full

kǒu
口：mouth

mǎn kǒu
满 口：always talk about

rén yì
仁义：virtue

dào dé
道德：morality,

mǎn kǒu rén yì dào dé
满口仁义道德：always talks about virtue and morality

yī
一：one

dù zi
肚子：stomach

yī dù zi
一肚子：always thinks of

nán
男：man

dào qiáng dào
盗 = 强盗：ruffian, robber

nǚ
女：women

chāng chāng jì
娼 = 娼妓：whore

yī dù zi nán dào nǚ chāng
一肚子男盗女娼：always thinks about the dirty things, as do ruffians and whores

指两面派人物，嘴上说的都是一些高尚的话，心里想的都是一些肮脏的事。

māo kū lǎo shǔ jiǎ cí bēi
猫 哭 老 鼠 假 慈 悲。

Proverb: A cat crying for a mouse is a fake mercy.

Comment: This proverb refers to people who pretend to sympathize with a victim.

māo
猫：cat

kū
哭：cry

lǎo shǔ
老 鼠：mouse

māo kū lǎo shǔ
猫 哭 老 鼠：a cat crrying for a mouse

jiǎ
假：fake

cí bēi
慈 悲：mercy

jiǎ cí bēi
假 慈 悲：fake mercy

mā kū lǎo shǔ jiǎ cí bēi
猫 哭 老 鼠 假 慈 悲：a cat crying for a mouse is a fake mercy

猫性食鼠，哭老鼠也是装样子给人看的。比喻假装同情受害者。

máo cè lǐ dē shí tou yòu chòu yòu yìng
茅 厕 里 的 石 头，又 臭 又 硬。

Proverb: A stone in the latrine, both stinky and hard.
Comment: This phrase refers to people who are not only bad but also stubborn.

máo cè
茅 厕：a Chinese style latrine

lǐ
里：inside

dē
的：'s

shí tou
石 头：stone

máo cè lǐ dē shí tou
茅 厕 里 的 石 头：a stone in the latrine

yòu
又：again, also

chòu
臭：stinking

yìng
硬：hard

yòu chòu yòu yìng
又 臭 又 硬：both stinky and hard

比喻某个人又坏又顽固。

méi chī guò zhū ròu hái méi jiàn guò zhū pǎo
没吃过猪肉，还没见过猪跑？

Proverb: If you have not eaten pig meat, have you seen pigs run yet?
Comment: If you haven't experienced something, at least you have seen it before and have some knowledge of it.

méi méi yǒu
没 = 没 有：not have

chī
吃：eat

guò
过：pass, have been

chī guò
吃 过：had eaten

zhū
猪：pig

ròu
肉：meat

méi chī guò zhū ròu
没 吃 过 猪 肉：have not eaten pig meat

hái
还：yet

jiàn
见：see

jiàn guò
见 过：have seen

hái méi jiàn guò
还 没 见 过：haven't seen yet

pǎo
跑：run

zhū pǎo
猪 跑：pigs run

hái méi jiàn guò zhū pǎo
还 没 见 过 猪 跑：have you seen pigs run yet

比喻对某些事情虽然没有亲身经历过，但还是看见过，知道其中的一二。

méi le tóu dē cāng yīng luàn zhuàng yī qì
没了头的苍蝇，乱撞一气。

Proverb: A fly without a head will be collide with anything it passes nonstop.

Comment: This saying is used to describe somebody who cannot control his behavior.

méi méi yǒu
没 = 没 有：not have, without

le
了：no meaning, used after an adjective to show a change is finished.

tóu
头：head

dē
的：'s

cāng yīng
苍 蝇：a fly

méi lē tóu dē cāng yīng
没了头的苍蝇：a fly without a head

luàn
乱：in disorder

zhuàng
撞：collide with

yī qì
一 气：one breath, non stop

luàn zhuàng yī qì
乱 撞 一气：collide with anything it passes nonstop

比喻人失去了主宰，不能控制自己的行为。

méi yǒu jiā guǐ yǐn bú jìn wài suì
没有家鬼，引不进外祟。

Proverb: If the family does not have its own ghost, there will be no ghost to let outside evil spirits in.

Comment: A family ghost refers to an insider who will betray the family. If there is no "family ghost," the family or group will be better off.

yǒu
有：have

méi yǒu
没有：not have

jiā
家：home, family

guǐ
鬼：ghost

jiā guǐ
家鬼：a family's ghost; here means a bad person in the family

méi yǒu jiā guǐ
没有家鬼：not have a family ghost

yǐn
引：lead

bú
不：no, not

jìn
进：into

yǐn jìn
引进：lead into

yǐn bú jìn
引不进：cannot lead in

wài   wài miàn
外 = 外面：outside

suì
祟：an evil spirit

yǐn bú jìn wài suì
引不进外祟：can't lead outside evil spirits in

家鬼：家里的活鬼，坏人。祟：妖精，也指不光彩的行为。没有坏人在里面做内应，外部势力就难以入侵，造成危害。

mín pà bīng fěi qiǎng guān pà shā mào diū
民怕兵匪抢，官怕纱帽丢，

qióng pà cháng shēng bìng fù pà zéi lái tōu
穷怕常生病，富怕贼来偷。

Proverb: People fear being robbed by soldiers or gangsters; officials fear losing their black gauze cap; poor people fear always being sick; rich people fear that a thief will come to steal.

Comment: A black gauze cap was worn by feudal officials. Once these officials lost their power, they could no longer wear the cap. Different people have their own things to fear.

mín rén míng bǎi xìn
民 = 人民，百姓：people; here means common people

pà
怕：fear, be afraid

bīng shì bīng
兵 = 士兵：soldier

fěi fěi tú
匪 = 匪徒：gangster

qiǎng qiǎng jié
抢 = 抢劫：rob

mín pà bīng fěi qiǎng
民怕兵匪抢：people fear being robbed by soldiers or gangsters

guān
官：official

mào mào zi
帽 = 帽子：hat

shā mào wū shā mào
纱 帽 = 乌 纱 帽：black gauze cap, made by black cotton yarn

diū shā mào diū
丢：lose 纱 帽 丢：lose black gauze cap; means be fired

guān pà shā mào diū
官 怕 纱 帽 丢：officials fear losing their black gauze cap

qióng
穷：poor; here means poor people

cháng jīng cháng
常 = 经 常：often, always

shēng bìng
生 病：sick

qióng pà cháng shēng bìng
穷 怕 常 生 病：poor people fear always being sick

fù
富：wealthy, rich; here means rich people

zéi
贼：thief

lái
来：come

tōu
偷：steal

fù pà zéi lái tōu
富 怕 贼 来 偷：rich people fear that a thief comes to steal

指各有所怕。

míng xiū zhàn dào àn dù chén cāng
明 修 栈 道，暗 渡 陈 仓。

Proverb: Construct a footway on the edge of a cliff in broad daylight; at the same time, send troops in secret to the country town Chen Cang to attack the enemy.
Comment: This refers to an ancient Chinese strategy of setting up a decoy to distract an opponent from the real purpose.

míng
明：bright, under the sun

xiū xiū jiàn
修 = 修 建：construct

zhàn dào
栈 道：a narrow footway planked over a cliff

míng xiū zhàn dào
明 修 栈 道：construct a footway on the high mountain in plain view

àn àn zhōng
暗 = 暗 中：secretly

dù
渡：pass through; here means attack

àn dù
暗 渡：attack secretly

chén cāng
陈 仓：a name of a country town

àn dù chén cāng
暗 渡 陈 仓：attack the country town Chen Cang secretly

栈道：古时在悬崖峭壁上凿开石头，用木头架起来的道路。
暗渡：偷偷地去做。陈仓：地名。表面上派兵修复栈道，装作要从栈道出击的姿态，实际上却暗中抄小路袭击陈仓。
比喻暗中活动，用假象迷惑别人，来达到自己的目的。

mō zhē shí tóu guò hé
摸 着 石 头 过 河。

Proverb: Cross the river by feeling the stones.

Comment: This means to proceed cautiously with a new venture. This proverb was used by Chinese leader Deng Xiaoping to describe China's new economic policy after the Cultural Revolution.

mō
摸：touch, feel

zhē
着：no meaning, to indicate action or status is continued

shí tóu
石 头：stone

guò
过：across

hé
河：river

guò hé
过 河：across the river

mō zhē shí tóu guò hé
摸 着 石 头 过 河：cross the river by feeling the stones

在对河的深浅不清楚的情况下，摸到河底的石头，找最安全的地方过河。指对从来没有做过的事情要一边摸索一边干，边干边总结经验，摸索着前进。

mǔ gǒu bú diào wěi gōng gǒu bú shàng shēn
母狗不掉尾，公狗不上身。

Proverb: If a bitch does not waggle her tail, a male dog cannot mount her.
Comment: If the woman does not show interest, the man cannot have sex.

mǔ
母：female

gǒu
狗：dog

bú
不：no, not

diào
掉：drip; here means waggle

wěi wěi ba
尾 = 尾 巴：tail

diào wěi
掉 尾：waggle tail

mǔ gǒu bú diào wěi
母 狗 不 掉 尾：a female dog not waggles her tail

gōng
公：male

gōng gǒu
公 狗：male dog

shàng
上：on top, mount

shēn shēn tǐ
身 = 身 体：body

gōng gǒu bú shàng shēn
公 狗 不 上 身：a male dog can not mount her

掉尾：翘起尾巴求欢。上身：爬上来交配。指男女通奸淫乱，女人不主动，男人很难达到目的。

mǔ	yǐ	zǐ	wéi	guì	qī	yǐ	fū	wéi	róng
母	以	子	为	贵，	妻	以	夫	为	荣。

Proverb: A mother can be more valuable because of her son; a wife can be proud of marrying a powerful husband.

Comment: In traditional China, man was the center of society. Women's status, wealth, and power were derived from their husbands and sons.

mǔ mǔ qīn
母 = 母 亲：mother

zǐ ér zi
子 = 儿 子：son

yǐ wéi
以……为：because of

guì
贵：expensive, valuable

mǒ yǐ zǐ wéi guì
母 以 子 为 贵：a mother can be more valuable because of her son

qī qī zi
妻 = 妻 子：wife

fū zhàng fū
夫 = 丈 夫：husband

róng róng yào
荣 = 荣 耀：proud of

qī yǐ fū wéi róng
妻 以 夫 为 荣：a wife can be proud of marrying a powerful husband

在以男人为中心的社会里，只有生了儿子，为家族传宗接代，才能确立在家庭的地位；也只有嫁了有权势的丈夫，才能享受荣华富贵。

mǔ dān huā xià sǐ zuò guǐ yě fēng liú
牡 丹 花 下 死，做 鬼 也 风 流。

Proverb: To die under a Mu Dan flower, even becoming a ghost, is still romantic.

Comment: A Mu Dan flower is a peony and is a symbol for a beautiful woman. Romance is worth dying for. The Mu Dan was very popular in traditional China, especially in the Qing Dynasty (1644–1911).

huā
花：flower

mǔ dān
牡 丹：peony

mǔ dān huā
牡 丹 花：a Mu Dan flower; here means a beautiful woman

xià
下：below, under

sǐ
死：die

mǔ dān huā xià sǐ
牡 丹 花 下 死：die under a peony

zuò
做：be; here means become

guǐ
鬼：host

yě
也：also

fēng liú
风 流：romantic

zuò guǐ yě fēng liú
做 鬼 也 风 流：even becoming a ghost is still romantic

牡丹花：比喻女人。风流：风韵，风情。这是冒死偷情者的口号。指为性事频繁而死，即使死了也是一种风流韵事，死得值得。

mù ǒu néng tiào dòng zì yǒu tí xiàn rén
木偶能跳动，自有提线人。

Proverb: A wooden puppet can jump and move around; of course, there is the person who pulls the strings.

Comment: If something unusual happens, there are always people behind the scenes manipulating things.

mù ǒu
木偶：wooden puppet

néng
能：can

tiào
跳：jump

dòng
动：make a movement

mù ǒu néng tiào dòng
木偶能跳动：a wooden puppet can jump and move around

zì　zì rán
自 = 自然：of course

yǒu
有：have

tí
提：lift, pull

xiàn
线：string

rén
人：a person

tí xiàn rén
提线人：a person person who pulls the strings

zì yǒu tí xiàn rén
自有提线人：of course, there is the person who pulls the strings

木头人之所以会表演，是由于有人在幕后提线操纵。比喻某种异常情况的出现或某些人的异常活动，背后一定有人指使操纵。

nǎ yǒu māo ér bù tōu xīng
哪 有 猫 儿 不 偷 腥。

Proverb: How can a cat not steal raw meat or fish?

Comment: People who are greedy and vicious will find it very difficult to change their behavior.

nǎ nǎ lǐ
哪 = 哪 里：where

yǒu
有：have

māo ér māo
猫 儿 = 猫：cat

bù
不：no, not

tōu
偷：steal

xīng
腥：raw meat or fish

tōu xīng
偷 腥：steal raw meat or fish

nǎ yǒu māo ér bù tōu xīng
哪 有 猫 儿 不 偷 腥：how can a cat not steal raw meat or fish

猫儿性喜吃鱼腥类食物，比喻贪婪邪恶的人习性难改。

nán pà rù cuò háng nǚ pà jià cuò láng
男怕入错行，女怕嫁错郎。

Proverb: A man is afraid of choosing the wrong occupation; a woman is afraid of marrying the wrong man.

Comment: In traditional China a woman's life depended on the man. Being married to the wrong man would be a disaster.

nán
男：a man, male

pà
怕：afraid

rù jìng rù
入 = 进 入：enter, go into

cuò
错：a mistake, faults

rù cuò
入 错：enter wrong

háng háng yè
行 = 行 业：occupation, profession

nán pà rù cuò háng
男 怕 入 错 行：a man is afraid of choosing the wrong occupation

nǚ
女：a woman, female

jià
嫁：marry

jià cuò
嫁 错：marry wrong

láng
郎：a man

nǚ pà jià cuò láng
女 怕 嫁 错 郎：a woman is afraid of marrying the wrong man

指男人最怕的是选错了职业，女人最怕选错了丈夫，过不上好日子。

nǐ zǒu nǐ dē yáng guān dào wǒ zǒu wǒ dē dú mù qiáo
你走你的阳关道，我走我的独木桥。

Proverb: You walk on your Yangguan Avenue; I walk on my single-plank bridge.
Comment: Yangguan Avenue was in old Dunhuang and had very heavy traffic. Dunhuang was a city on the old Silk Road. This proverb means, "You go your way; I go my way. Good-bye."

nǐ
你：you

zǒu
走：walk

nǐ dē
你 的：your

yáng guān
阳 关：Yang Guan, a place's name

dào
道：an avenue

yáng guān dào
阳 关 道：Yang Guan Avenue, a heavy traffic place in Dun Huang

nǐ zǒu nǐ dē yáng guān dào
你走你的阳 关 道：you walk on your Yang Guan Avenue

wǒ
我：I, me

wǒ dē
我 的：my

dú
独：one and only

mù
木：wood

qiáo
桥：bridge

dú mù qiáo
独 木 桥：a single plank bridge

wǒ zǒu wǒ dē dú mù qiáo
我 走 我的独木 桥：I walk on my single plank bridge

阳关故址在今甘肃敦煌西南，当初是车水马龙的阳关大道。这是中国人在绝交时讲的话，指你我关系断绝，各奔前程。

nìng féng è bīn wù féng gù rén
宁 逢 恶 宾，勿 逢 故 人。

Proverb: Rather run into an evil visitor than an old friend or acquaintance.
Comment: An old friend or acquaintance knows your personal history, including things you don't want revealed.

nìng nìng kě
宁 = 宁 可：rather

féng yù dào
逢 = 遇 到：run into

è
恶：evil

bīn bīn kè
宾 = 宾 客：guests or visitor

nìng féng è bīn
宁 逢 恶 宾：rather run into a evil visitor

wù bú yào
勿 = 不 要：don't

wù féng
勿 逢：not run into

gù yǐ qián dē
故 = 以 前 的：former, old

rén
人：people

gù rén
故 人：old friends or acquaintance

wù féng gù rén
勿 逢 故 人：rather not run into an old friend or acquaintance

宁愿碰上一个难对付的凶恶宾客，也不愿碰上一个知道自己老底的老朋友。指怕老朋友揭底。

宁借人停丧 不借人成双
張

nìng jiè rén tíng sàng bú jiè rén chéng shuāng
宁 借 人 停 丧，不 借 人 成 双。

Proverb: Rather lend people a room to park a coffin than lend a couple the room for a wedding.

Comment: The coffin is bad luck, but it is there only a short time. If a couple is married in your house, they might have a baby and never leave.

nìng nìng kě
宁 = 宁 可：rather

jiè
借：lend

rén
人：people

jiè rén
借 人：lend people

nìng jiè rén
宁 借 人：rather lend people

tíng tíng fàng
停 = 停 放：park

sàng
丧：funeral

tíng sàng
停 丧：park a coffin

nìng jiè rén tíng sàng
宁 借 人 停 丧：rather lend people a room to park a coffin

bú
不：not

bú jiè rén
不 借 人：not lend people

chéng
成：become

shuāng
双：two, twin, both

chéng shuāng
成 双：become two; here means have a wedding

bú jiè rén chéng shuāng
不 借 人 成 双：not lend a couple the room for a wedding

停丧：安葬前把灵柩暂时停放在某处。成双：指办理婚事。停丧时间短，借出的房子能很快收回；婚事办成之后，很可能在你这里安家了。

nìng wéi jī shǒu wù wéi niú hòu

宁为鸡首，勿为牛后。

Proverb: Rather be a chicken's head than a cow's butt.

Comment: It's better to be a big fish in a small pond. The Chinese Proverb is obviously a bit more colorful than the English version.

nìng nìng kě
宁 = 宁 可：rather

wéi chéng wéi
为 = 成 为：be, become

níng wéi
宁 为：rather be

jī
鸡：chicken

shǒu
首：first, head

jī shǒu
鸡 首：chicken's head

níng wéi jī shǒu
宁 为 鸡 首：rather be a chicken's head

wù bú yào
勿 = 不 要：don't

wù wéi
勿 为：don't be

niú
牛：cow

hòu
后：back; here means cow's tail

wù wéi niú hòu
勿 为 牛 后：not be cow's tail

比喻宁愿在小地方做个有实权的风光人物，也不愿意在大场合听从更有权势的人的使唤。

ning yawn du tou yi zhi ji bu yuan he tou yi tou niu
宁愿独偷一只鸡，不愿合偷一头牛。

Proverb: Rather steal a chicken by yourself than steal a cow with others.
Comment: He who works alone works best.

ning yuan
宁愿：rather

du
独：alone

tou
偷：steal

yi
一：one

zhi
只：a measure word for chicken

ji
鸡：chicken

yi zhi ji
一只鸡：a chicken

ning yuan du tou yi zhi ji
宁愿独偷一只鸡：rather steal a chicken by yourself

bu
不：not

bu yuan
不愿：rather not

he he zuo
合 = 合作：cooperate

he tou
合偷：steal together

tou
头：a measure word for cow

niu
牛：cow

yi tou niu
一头牛：a cow

bu yuan he tou yi tou niu
不愿合偷一头牛：rather not steal a cow with others

指如果要谋利的话，与其与人合作，还不如单干。即使利益小一点，也是自己独得。

niú	tóu	shēn	dào	mǎ	cáo	lǐ
牛	头	伸	到	马	槽	里。

Proverb: A cow's head stretched out into a horse's manger.
Comment: Some people come to other people's territory to gain benefits.

niú
牛：cow

tóu
头：head

niú tóu
牛 头：cow's head

shēn
伸：stretch

dào
到：reach

shēn dào
伸 到：stretch out into

mǎ
马：horse

cáo
槽：manger

lǐ　　lǐ miàn
里 = 里 面：inside

mǎ cáo lǐ
马 槽 里：inside of the horse's manger

niú tóu shēn dào mǎ cáo lǐ
牛 头 伸 到 马 槽 里：a cow's head stretched out into a horse's manger

比喻到不是自己的领域里去捞取好处。

nǚ rén tōu rén gē céng zhǐ nán rén tōu rén gē zuò shān
女人偷人隔层纸，男人偷人隔座山。

Proverb: When a woman commits adultery, between the man and woman there is only a piece of paper; when a man commits adultery, there is a mountain between the man and the woman.
Comment: If a woman wants to have sex, it's easy to find a man. If a man wants to have sex, it is more difficult to find a woman.

nǚ
女：female

rén
人：people, a person

nǚ rén
女人：woman

tōu
偷：steal

tōu rén
偷人：adultery

gē
隔：separated

céng
层：a measure word for paper

zhǐ
纸：paper

nǚ rén tōu rén gē céng zhǐ
女人偷人隔层纸：when woman commits adultery, between the man and woman there is only a piece of paper

nán
男：male

nán nán rén
男 = 男人：man

zuò
座：a measure word for mountain

shān
山：mountain

nán rén tōu rén gē zuò shān
男人偷人隔座山：when a man commits adultery, there is a mountain between the man and the woman

指男女之情，若男人主动，成事比较困难，就像中间隔了一座大山；若女人主动，就像捅破一层纸那样容易，意思是：想干什么就可以干什么。

pǎo dé liǎo hé shàng pǎo bù liǎo miào
跑得了和尚跑不了庙。

Proverb: The monk can run away but the temple cannot.

Comment: A person can flee, but his property must remain behind.

pǎo
跑：run

pǎo dé liǎo
跑得了：can run away

hé shàng
和尚：monk

pǎo dé liǎo hé shàng
跑得了和尚：the monk can run away

bù
不：no, not

pǎo bù liǎo
跑不了：can not run away

miào
庙：temple

pǎo bù liǎo miào
跑不了庙：the temple cannot run away

和尚有脚，出了事可以逃跑，但庙是不动产。比喻即使当事人逃跑了，但与他关联的人或财物都跑不了。指事情既然已经出了，终究是逃不脱，躲不过的。

pí	fú	hàn	dà	shù	kě	xiào	bú	zì	liàng
蚍	蜉	撼	大	树，	可	笑	不	自	量。

Proverb: The big ant tries to shake the big tree, which is very funny because it overestimates its own strength.

Comment: Used to laugh at people who overestimate their own power.

pí fú　dà mǎ yǐ
蚍 蜉 = 大 蚂 蚁：big ant

hàn　yáo hàn
撼 = 摇 撼：shake

dà
大：big

shù
树：tree

pí fú hàn dà shù
蚍 蜉 撼 大 树：the big ant shakes the big tree

xiào
笑：laugh

kě xiào
可 笑：funny

bú
不：not

zì　zì jǐ
自 = 自 己：self

liàng　gū liàng
量 = 估 量：estimate

zì liàng
自 量：self estimate

kě xiào bú zì liàng
可 笑 不 自 量：very funny because it overestimates its own strength

蚍蜉：大蚂蚁。大蚂蚁力量微小，却妄图动摇高大的树木。经常用来比喻人盲目自大，不自量力做些力所不能及的事。

qī shí bù liú sù bā shí bù liú cān
七十不留宿，八十不留餐。

Proverb: Do not urge a seventy-year-old to stay overnight; do not urge an eighty-year-old to stay and have a meal.

Comment: A seventy-year-old might have an accident sleeping. And eighty-years-old might have an accident eating.

qī
七：seven

shí
十：ten

qī shí
七十：seventy

bù
不：no, not

liú wǎn liú
留 = 挽留：urge someone stay, not to leave

sù zhù sù
宿 = 住宿：stay overnight

qī shí bù liú sù
七十不留宿：do not urge a seventy-year-old to stay overnight

bā
八：eight

bā shí
八十：eighty

cān
餐：a meal

liú cān
留餐：ask someone to stay and have a meal

bā shí bù liú cān
八十不留餐：do not ask an eighty-year-old to stay and have a meal

七十岁的人睡觉会发生意外，八十岁的人连吃饭也会发生意外，因此不要挽留。指年纪老的人容易发生意外，最好少和他们来往。

qī bù rú qiè qiè bù rú tōu tōu dē zháo hái bù rú tōu bù zháo
妻不如妾，妾不如偷，偷得着还不如偷不着。

Proverb: A wife is not as good as a concubine; a concubine is not as good as having an affair; having an affair is not as good as the anticipation of having an affair.
Comment: A man will always be attracted by a new woman.

qī
妻：wife

bù rú
不如：not as good as

qiè
妾：concubine

qī bù rú qiè
妻不如妾：a wife is not as good as a concubine

tōu
偷：steal; here means having an affair

qiè bù rú tōu
妾不如偷：concubine is not as good as to having an affair

tōu dē zháo
偷得着：having had an affair

hái
还：still

hái bù rú
还不如：still not as good as

tōu bù zháo
偷不着：can not have an affair; here means anticipation of having an affair

tōu dē zháo hái bù rú tōu bù zháo
偷得着还不如偷不着：having had an affair is not as good as the anticipation of having an affair

指一种偷情的心理状态，人总是被新鲜事物所引诱。

qiān lǐ zhī dī kuì yú yī yǐ zhī xuè
千里之堤，溃于一蚁之穴。

Proverb: A five-hundred-kilometer dam breaks because of one ant's nest.
Comment: Sometimes little things can turn into big disasters

qiān
千：thousand

lǐ
里：a unit of Chinese length equal to half kilometer

qiān lǐ
千 里：five hundred kilometer

zhī
之：'s

dī dī bà
堤 = 堤 坝：dam

qiān lǐ zhī dī
千 里 之 堤：a five-hundred-kilometer dam; here means very long dam

kuì kuì jué
溃 = 溃 决：break

yú
于：in, at, on, by, from

yī
一：one

yǐ mǎ yǐ
蚁 = 蚂 蚁：ant

yī yǐ
一 蚁：an ant

xuè
穴：nest

kuì yú yī yǐ zhī xuè
溃 于 一 蚁 之 穴：breaks because of one ant's nest

千里长堤由于未堵一个小小的蚂蚁洞而遭到溃决。比喻小事不慎，可以酿成大祸。

qián rén zāi shù hòu rén chéng liáng
前 人 栽 树， 后 人 乘 凉。

Proverb: The earlier generation plants the tree; the later generations relax in the cool shade of the tree.
Comment: Later generations benefit from the earlier generations' hard work and labor.

qián
前：front

rén
人：people, a person

qián rén
前 人：earlier generation

zāi
栽：plant

shù
树：a tree

zāi shù
栽 树：plan a tree

qián rén zāi shù
前 人 栽 树：the earlier generation plants the tree

hòu
后：behind, after, later

hòu rén
后 人：later generations

chéng
乘：ride

liáng
凉：cool

chéng liáng
乘 凉：relax in a cool place; here means the shade of the tree

hòu rén chéng liáng
后 人 乘 凉：the later generations relax in the cool shade of the tree

先人栽下的树苗，长成大树后，后辈在树下乘凉，比喻前人为后人造福。

qiāng dǎ chū tóu niǎo
枪 打 出 头 鸟。

Proverb: The gun always shoots the bird with its head stuck out.
Comment: The best way to stay out of trouble is not to be noticed.

qiāng
枪：gun

dǎ
打：hit; here means shoots

chū
出：stick out

tóu
头：head

chū tóu
出 头：the head sticks out

niǎo
鸟：bird

chū tóu niǎo
出 头 鸟：the bird with the head stuck out

qiāng dǎ chū tóu niǎo
枪 打 出 头 鸟：gun shoots the bird with its head stuck out

指冲在第一线的，总是成为首先被打击的对象。

qiáng lóng dòu bú guò dì tóu shé
强 龙 斗 不 过 地 头 蛇。

Proverb: A powerful dragon can’t win against a snake in its own territory.

Comment: Powerful people from the outside are at a disadvanantage when they are not in their own territory.

qiáng
强：strong, powerful

lóng
龙：dragon

qiáng lóng
强 龙：powerful dragon

dòu
斗：fight

bú
不：no, not

guò
过：pass, over

dòu bú guò
斗 不 过：can’t win

dòu dé guò
斗 得 过：can win

shé
蛇：a snake

dì tóu shé
地 头 蛇：a snake in its own territory

qiáng lóng dòu bú guò dì tóu shé
强 龙 斗不过地头蛇：a powerful dragon can’t win against a snake in its own territory

地头蛇：地方上恶霸，坏人。比喻外来的强手也斗不过当地的恶势力。

qiáng niǔ dē guā bù tián
强扭的瓜不甜。

Proverb: Pick a melon by twisting the stem with force, and the melon will not be sweet.
Comment: If you force someone to do something before he is ready, the results will never be as good as if he did it voluntarily.

qiáng
强：strong; here means by force

niǔ
扭：turn around, twist

dē
的：'s

qiáng niǔ dē
强 扭 的：pluck by twisting with force

guā
瓜：melon

bù
不：no, not

tián
甜：sweet

bù tián
不 甜：not sweet

qiáng niǔ dē guā bù tián
强 扭 的 瓜 不 甜：pick a melon by twisting the stem with force and the melon will not be sweet

强：勉强。瓜未成熟而强摘下来，自然不会香甜。比喻非出于自愿，而是用强制的手段去勉强行事，效果不会好。

qiǎo mèi yǎn zuò gě xiā zi kàn
巧 媚 眼 做 给 瞎 子 看。

Proverb: Make a cute, sexy glance at a blind person.

Comment: This phrase means to waste time and effort on someone who doesn't even know that you are doing it.

qiǎo
巧：cute

mèi wú mèi
媚 = 妩 媚：sexy and charming

yǎn
眼：eye

mèi yǎn
媚 眼：a sexy glance

qiǎo mèi yǎn
巧 媚 眼：a cute, sexy glance

zuò
做：make

gěi
给：give

xiā zi
瞎 子：a blind person

kàn
看：see

qiǎo mèi yǎn zuò gěi xiā zi kàn
巧 媚 眼 做 给 瞎 子 看：make a cute, sexy glance at a blind person

指下了很多功夫做的事情，可惜对方看不到，白费劲。

qiè gōu zhě zhū qiè guó zhě hóu
窃 钩 者 诛，窃 国 者 侯。

Proverb: A petty thief who steals the hook of a clothing bag is executed; a big thief who steals the country will have a noble title conferred on him.
Comment: The law can be unfair.

qiè
窃：steal

gōu
钩：a hook of a clothing bag

zhě
者：a person

qiè gōu zhě
窃 钩 者：a person who steals a hook

zhū shā diào
诛 = 杀 掉：execute

qiè gōu zhě zhū
窃 钩 者 诛：a thief who steals the hook of a clothing bag is executed

guó guó jiā
国 = 国 家：country

qiè guó zhě
窃 国 者：a person who steals the country

hóu fēng hóu
侯 = 封 侯：a noble title; here means confer a noble title

qiè guó zhě hóu
窃 国 者 侯：a thief who steals the country will have a noble title conferred upon him

侯：封为贵族。偷窃衣袋钩的小贼，抓住了就要被处死。窃取国家权柄的大盗却可以被封为贵族。指出法律常常是不公平的。西方人也有类似的说法：偷了一片面包，把你送进监狱。偷了一条铁路，把你送进国会。

qíng rén yǎn lǐ chū xī shī
情 人 眼 里 出 西 施。

Proverb: From a lover's eye, even an ordinary woman comes out as beautiful as Xi Shi.

Comment: Xi Shi was one of the Four Beauties of ancient China. Xi Shi's beauty was said to be so extreme that while leaning over a balcony to look at the fish in a pond, the fish would be so dazzled that they forgot to swim. The fish would gradually sink away from the surface, the birds would forget to fly and fallfrom the sky, the moon would fade, and the flowers would close their petals in shame in comparison with her.

qíng rén
情 人：lover

yǎn
眼：eye

lǐ
里：inside

yǎn lǐ
眼 里：from his eye

chū
出：exit, come out

xī shī
西 施：most beautiful women in history, symbol of beauty

chū xī shī
出 西 施：come out a most beautiful women Xi Shi

qíng rén yǎn lǐ chū xī shī
情 人 眼 里 出 西 施：from a lover's eye even an ordinary woman comes out as beautiful as Xi Shi

情人：指相爱中的人。西施：中国古代美女，后来作为美女的代称。男子对于自己钟情的女子，即使相貌平常，也会觉得像西施一样美。比喻感情用事，把认识的主观性绝对化。

qǐng shén róng yì sòng shén nán
请神容易送神难。

Proverb: Inviting a god to come in is easy; getting rid of him is difficult.

Comment: If you get help from someone and they don't get what they think they deserve, they will be difficult to get rid of.

qǐng
请：invite

shén
神：deity, god; here means a person

róng yì
容易：easy, simple

qǐng shén róng yì
请神容易：Inviting a god to come in is easy

sòng
送：give as a present, or send someone out; here means getting rid of

nán
难：difficult

sòng shén nán
送神难：getting rid of him is difficult

神：提供外援的人。请人帮忙不是没有代价的，一旦请进来而没有给他相当的报酬，想再要摆脱他就非常困难。

qióng suàn mìng fù shāo xiāng
穷 算 命，富 烧 香。

Proverb: Poor people see the fortune-teller; rich people burn joss sticks.

Comment: Poor people want the fortune-teller to tell them their fate. Rich people burn joss sticks to beg Buddha to bless and protect their wealth forever.

qióng
穷：poor; here means poor people

suàn mìng
算 命：fortune-telling

qióng suàn mìng
穷 算 命：poor people see the fortune-teller

fù
富：rich, wealthy

shāo xiāng
烧 香：burn joss sticks

fù shāo xiāng
富 烧 香：rich people burn joss sticks

穷人爱算命，希望知道命运何时有转机，希望摆脱贫困；富人爱烧香拜佛，祈求神保佑自己永远富贵。

rén duō lǎn lóng duō hàn jī duō bú xià dàn
人 多 懒，龙 多 旱，鸡 多 不 下 蛋。

Proverb: The more people there are, the lazier they get; the more dragons there are, the drier the weather; the more chickens, the fewer the eggs.
Comment: When there are more people, nobody takes responsibility. As far as dragons go, Chinese traditionally believed dragons suck the water from the river and then spit the water out as rain. When there are too many dragons, the dragons get lazy, and there is no rain. The same with the chickens. Too many chickens, no eggs.

rén
人：people

duō
多：many, much

lǎn
懒：lazy

rén dūo lǎn
人 多 懒：when many people get together, people will be lazy

lóng
龙：dragon

lóng duō
龙 多：many dragons

hàn gān hàn
旱 = 干 旱：drought

lóng duō hàn
龙 多 旱：more dragons, then a drought

jī
鸡：chicken

jī duō
鸡 多：more chickens

bú
不：not

xià diàn
下 蛋：lay eggs

jī duō bú xià diàn
鸡 多 不 下 蛋：more chickens not lay eggs

比喻人虽少，但责任明确，事情容易办成。人多了，责任不明确，反而办不成事。

rén jí xuán liáng gǒu jí tiào qiáng
人急悬梁，狗急跳墙。

Proverb: Put people under heavy pressure, and they will hang themselves from the roof beam; put pressure on a dog, and it will jump over the wall.
Comment: Don't push people too hard.

rén
人：a person, people

jí　bī jí
急 = 逼急：under heavy pressure

xuán　xuán guà
悬 = 悬挂：hang

liáng　fáng liáng
梁 = 房梁：roof beam

xuán liáng
悬梁：hang self from the roof beam; here means to commit suicide

rén jí xuán liáng
人急悬梁：put people under heavy pressure, they will hang themselves from the roof beam

gǒu
狗：dog

tiào
跳：jump

qiáng
墙：wall

tiào qiáng
跳墙：jump over the wall

gǒu jí tiào qiáng
狗急跳墙：put pressure on a dog, and it will jump over the wall

悬梁：在房梁上上吊自尽。人被逼急了就会以死相拼，上吊自杀；狗被逼急了会跳上墙去。指人被逼到走投无路时，就会不顾一切地去蛮干。比喻不可逼人太甚，走上绝路，对双方无益。

rén pà chū míng zhū pà zhuàng
人 怕 出 名 猪 怕 壮。

Proverb: People are afraid to be well known, just like a pig is afraid to be stout and strong.

Comment: When the pig gets fat, it's time to kill the pig and send it to market. Well-known people attract troubles.

rén
人：a person, people

pà
怕：afraid

chū míng
出 名：famous, well-known

rén pà chū míng
人 怕 出 名：people are afraid to be well-known

zhū
猪：pig

zhū pà
猪 怕：pig is afraid

zhuàng féi zhuàng
壮 = 肥 壮：stout and strong

zhū pà zhuàng
猪 怕 壮：pig is afraid to be stout and strong

人出名了就招人嫉妒，猪养肥了就要被宰杀。指人出了名就会招来麻烦。

rén qióng zhì duǎn mǎ shòu máo cháng
人 穷 志 短，马 瘦 毛 长。

Proverb: If a person is poor, his ambition is low. If a horse is skinny, his hair looks longer.
Comment: When people are poor, the first thing they worry about is having enough food to eat and clothes to keep warm. Horses all have hair the same length, but a skinny horse's hair will always looks longer. Used to laugh at some small-minded person who has no dream and ambition.

rén
人：a person, people

qióng
穷：poor

rén qióng
人 穷：when people is poor

zhì zhì qì
志 = 志 气：ambition

duǎn
短：short

rén qióng zhì duǎn
人 穷 志 短：if a people is poor, his ambition is low

mǎ
马：horse

shòu
瘦：skinny

máo
毛：hair, feather

cháng
长：long

mǎ shòu máo cháng
马 瘦 毛 长：if a horse is skinny, his hair looks longer

人穷了志向就只顾着吃饱穿暖而没了志向，就像马一样，马毛原本一样长，瘦马的毛看起来就显得特别长。

rén suī yǒu qiān suàn tiān zhǐ yǒu yī suàn
人虽有千算，天只有一算，

tiān ruò róng rén suàn shì shàng wú qióng hàn
天若容人算，世上无穷汉。

Proverb: Even if people calculate a thousand times, God only decides once; if God allowed people to decide their lives, there would be no poor Chinese man in this world.

Comment: Chinese believe that if a man is predestined to be poor by fate, no matter how hard he tries, he still cannot change his life.

rén
人：a person, people

suī　suī rán
虽 = 虽然：even if

yǒu
有：have

suī yǒu
虽有：even if

qiān
千：thousand

suàn　jì suàn
算 = 计算：calculate

rén suī yǒu qiān suàn
人虽有千算：even if people calculate a thousand times

tiān
天：sky; here means god

zhǐ
只：only

yǒu
有：have

yī
一：one

yī suàn
一算：one calculate

tiān zhǐ yǒu yī suàn
天只有一算：god only calculate once

ruò　tǎng ruò
若 = 倘若：if, suppose

róng　róng xǔ
容 = 允许：allow

tiān ruò róng rén suàn
天若容人算：if god allowed people to calculate

shì　shì jiè
世 = 世界：world

shàng
上：above, on top of

shì shàng
世上：in the world

wú　méi yǒu
无 = 没有：not have, without

qióng
穷：poor

hàn
汉：the Han Chinese race

qióng hàn
穷汉：a poor Chinese man

shì shàng wú qióng hàn
世上无穷汉：there would be no poor Chinese man in this world

指人穷是命中注定，再怎么计算也是改变不了的。

rén wú héng cái bú fù mǎ wú yě cǎo bù féi
人无横财不富，马无野草不肥。

Proverb: If people don't have a windfall, they cannot be rich; if a horse doesn't eat wild grass, the horse cannot be fat.
Comment: In ancient China, horses were fed straw at home. The horse would grow fat only if he could eat wild grass. So too, people couldn't get rich on their regular salary but needed to get some kind of windfall.

rén
人：a person, people

wú　méi yǒu
无 = 没 有：not have

héng cái
横 财：windfall, easy money

bú
不：no, not

fù
富：rich

bú fù
不 富：not rich

rén wú hén cái bú fù
人无横财不富：if people don't have a windfall, they cannot be rich

mǎ
马：horse

yě
野：wild

cǎo
草：grass, straw

yě cǎo
野草：wild grass

féi
肥：fat

bù féi
不 肥：not fat, thin

mǎ wú yě cǎo bù féi
马无野草不肥：if a horse doesn't eat wild grass, the horse cannot be fat

出自《增广贤文》。横财：意外之财。指人没有横财就富不起来，就像马不吃百家草就不长膘一样。

rén yào dǎo méi hē liáng shuǐ yě sāi yá
人要倒霉，喝凉水也塞牙。

Proverb: If a person has bad luck, even if he drinks cold water, the water will stick in his teeth.
Comment: Everything a person does turns into a disaster.

rén
人：a person, people

yào yào shì
要 = 要是：if

dǎo méi
倒霉：have bad luck

rén yào dǎo méi
人要倒霉：if a person has bad luck

hē
喝：drink

liáng
凉：cold

shuǐ
水：water

yě
也：also

sāi dǔ sāi
塞 = 堵塞：stick in

yá
牙：tooth

sāi yá
塞牙：stick something in the teeth

hē liáng shuǐ yě sāi yá
喝凉水也塞牙：even if he drinks cold water, the water will stick in his teeth

本来喝水是没问题的，但当一个人不走运时，不成问题的事也会成问题。比喻倒霉败兴。

rén yī zǒu chá jiù liáng
人 一 走，茶 就 凉。

Proverb: The person just left; his tea has gotten cold.

Comment: Once someone leaves a position or dies, his influence will weaken or disappear.

rén
人：a person, people

yī
一：one; here means once

zǒu zǒu kāi
走 = 走 开：leave

yī zǒu
一 走：once just left

rén yī zǒu
人 一 走：once the person just left

chá
茶：tea

jiù
就：be going to

liáng
凉：cold; here means getting cold

chá jiù liáng
茶 就 凉：the tea has gotten cold

是一种感慨，指人一离开，影响力削弱了甚至没有了，感情就淡薄了。多用来怪人没有情谊。

ròu	bāo	zi	dǎ	gǒu	yǒu	qù	wú	huí
肉	包	子	打	狗，	有	去	无	回。

Proverb: Hit a dog with a meat-stuffed bun, and the bun will not be coming back.
Comment: The dog will eat the bun. Things that are taken will not be given back.

ròu
肉：meat

bāo zi
包 子：steamed bun

ròu bāo zi
肉 包 子：steamed meat-stuffed bun

dǎ
打：hit

gǒu
狗：dog

ròu bāo zi dǎ gǒu
肉 包 子 打 狗：throw a steamed meat-stuffed bun to a dog

yǒu
有：have

qù
去：go

wú méi yǒu
无 = 没 有：not have

huí
回：return back

yǒu qù wú huí
有 去 无 回：only go, not return back

肉包子：有肉馅的包子。用肉的包子打狗，结果包子被狗吃了，拿不回来了，比喻一去不返。多用来说东西拿出去就再也收不回来了。

rú yú yǐn shuǐ lěng nuǎn zì zhī
如鱼饮水，冷暖自知。

Proverb: As the fish drinks the water, the fish knows whether the water's temperature is cold or warm.
Comment: In life, only the person who is involved knows what is really going on.

rú　rú tóng
如 = 如同：as

yú
鱼：fish

yǐn
饮：drink

shǐ
水：water

rú yú yǐn shuǐ
如鱼饮水：as a fish drinks the water

lěng
冷：cold

nuǎn
暖：warm

zì　zì jǐ
自 = 自己：oneself

zhī　zhī dào
知 = 知道：know

zì zhī
自知：oneself knows

léng nuǎn zì zhī
冷暖自知：the fish knows if the water's temperature is cold or warm

指做事情的甘苦，只有当事人自己知道。

rù guó wèn jìn rù jìng wèn sú
入国问禁，入境问俗。

Proverb: Ask for the taboos when you enter another country; ask for the local customs when you enter a new place.

Comment: You will make trouble because you don't know the local custom.

rù jìng rù
入 = 进 入：enter

guó guó jiā
国 = 国 家：door

wèn
问：ask for

jìn jìn jì
禁 = 禁 忌：prohibited, a taboo

wèn jìn
问 禁：ask for the taboos

rù guó wèn jìn
入 国 问 禁：ask for the taboos when you enter an another country

jìng huán jìng
境 = 环 境：circumstances

rù jìng
入 境：enter a new place

sú fēng sú
俗 = 风 俗：local custom

wèn sú
问 俗：ask for the local customs

rù jìng wèn sú
入 境 问 俗：ask for the local customs when you enter a new place

禁：禁忌。境：环境，地方。到一个国家或新的地方，先要搞清楚有什么禁忌，了解当地的风俗习惯，以免惹出麻烦。

ruò mén xiū wèn róng kū shì guān kàn róng yán biàn dé zhī
入门休问荣枯事，观看容颜便得知。

Proverb: When you enter the house, don't ask people whether business is good or bad; just look at the host's face, and you know what is going on.
Comment: People's moods, whether they are poor or rich, all show on their faces.

rù 入：enter　mén 门：door　rù mén 入门：enter the house

xiū bú yào 休 = 不要：do not　wèn 问：ask

róng fán róng 荣 = 繁荣：prosperous　kū kū jié 枯 = 枯竭：exhausted, out of luck

shì 事：things　róng kū shì 荣枯事：business is good or bad

rù mén xiū wèn róng kū shì
入门休问荣枯事：when you enter the house, don't ask people if business is good or bad

guān kàn 观看：look at　róng yán 容颜：facial appearance

biàn 便：thereupon　dé zhī 得知：know

guān kàn róng yán biàn dé zhī
观看容颜便得知：just look at the host's face and you know what is going on

荣：繁荣昌盛，指走运。枯：枯竭，指倒霉。容颜：容貌的颜色，指气色。进门不用问人家处境好坏，只要看主人的气色和表情就能知晓。指人的境遇和心情会在脸面上表现出来。

sài wēng shī mǎ yān zhī fēi fú
塞 翁 失 马，焉 知 非 福。

Proverb: The old man from the frontier fortress lost his horse; how do you know this is not a good fortune?
Comment: This is an old Chinese story. An old man from a frontier fortress had a good horse, but he lost it. A few days later, the horse came back and brought another good horse. The old man's son rode on the new horse but fell down and broke his leg. As a result, he had a limp and could not be conscripted into the army to fight in the war. Good fortune or bad fortune can be switched.

sài
塞：the frontier fortress

wēng
翁：an old man

sài wēng
塞 翁：old man from the frontier fortress

shī
失：lose

mǎ
马：horse

shī mǎ
失 马：lost his horse

yān
焉：how

zhī zhī dào
知 = 知 道：know

yān zhī
焉 知：how can you know

fēi
非：is not

fú
福：good fortune

fēi fú
非 福：not a good fortune

yān zhī fēi fú
焉 知 非 福：how do you know this is not a good fortune

塞北的老翁走失了一匹好马，不久马不仅自己回来了，还带回一匹好马。老翁的儿子骑了这匹新来的马跌断了腿。腿伤没好就遇到打仗要征兵，老翁的儿子正因为残疾而逃过一劫。因此说福祸是可以互相转化的。

三天不打
上房揭瓦

sān	tiān	bù	dǎ	shàng	fáng	jiē	wǎ
三	天	不	打，	上	房	揭	瓦。

Proverb: If you don't beat the children for three days, they will climb on the house and peel off the roof tiles.

Comment: This reflects the traditional Chinese approach to child rearing. If parents do not use physical punishment, the children will run wild.

sān
三：three

tiān
天：day

sān tiān
三 天：three days

bù
不：no, not

dǎ
打：beat

bù dǎ
不 打：not beat

sān tiān bù dǎ
三 天 不 打：don't beat the children for three days

shàng pá shàng
上 = 爬 上：climb up

fáng fáng zi
房 = 房 子：house

shàng fáng
上 房：will climb on the house

jiē jiē kāi
揭 = 揭 开：peel off

wǎ wǎ piàn
瓦 = 瓦 片：roof tile

jiē wǎ
揭 瓦：peel off the roof tiles

shàng fáng jiē wǎ
上 房 揭 瓦：they will climb on the house and peel off the roof tiles

这是中国人管教顽皮的小孩子时说的话，父母往往采取体罚的方式，认为不严加管教，小孩更会闹得无法无天。

sán dài fù guì shǐ zhī yǐn shí
三 代 富 贵 始 知 饮 食。

Proverb: After you have wealth and social position for three generations, then you start to know how to drink and eat.

Comment: Only families that are rich for a long time know how to enjoy life.

sān
三：three

dài
代：generation

fù
富：wealth

guì
贵：expensive, valued

fù guì
富 贵：wealth and social position

sān dài fù guì
三 代 富 贵：after you have wealth and social position for three generations

shǐ kāi shǐ
始 = 开 始：start

zhī zhī dào
知 = 知 道：know

yǐn
饮：drink

shí
食：eat or food

yǐn shí
饮 食：drink and eat food

shǐ zhī yǐn shí
始 知 饮 食：then you start to know how to drink and eat

世代富贵的人家而不是爆发户，才能真正懂生活的品位。

sān suì kàn dà qī suì kàn lǎo
三 岁 看 大，七 岁 看 老。

Proverb: Look at a three-year-old boy, and you can tell what he will look like when he grows up; look at a seven-year-old boy, and you can tell what he will look like when he is very old.
Comment: This is really about shaping a child's character for his or her whole life. The English expression would be "As the twig is bent so grows the tree."

sān
三：three

suì
岁：year old

sān suì
三 岁：three years old

kàn
看：look at

dà zhǎng dá
大 = 长 大：when he grows up

kàn dà
看 大：can tell what he will look like when he grows up

sān suì kàn dà
三 岁 看 大：look at a three-year-old boy, and you can tell what he will look like when he grows up

qī
七：seven

qī suì
七 岁：seven years old

lǎo
老：old

kàn lǎo
看 老：tell when he is very old

qī suì kàn lǎo
七 岁 看 老：look at a seven-year-old boy, and you can tell what he will look like when he is very old

儿童的言行就可预示他们成年后的性格。一个人在幼小成长发育阶段形成的自我个性，会影响到他未来的一生。

山中无老虎猴子称大王
酒

shān zhōng wú lǎo hǔ hóu zi chēng dà wáng
山　中　无老虎，猴　子　称　大　王。

Proverb: When the tiger is off the mountain, the monkey is king.
Comment: In English we might say when the cat's away, the mice will play.

sān
山：mountain

zhōng
中：inside

sān zhōng
山　中：in the mountains

wú
无：without

lǎo hǔ
老 虎：tiger

wú lǎo hǔ
无 老 虎：without tiger

shān zhōng wú lǎo hǔ
山　中　无老虎：when the tiger is off the mountain

hóu zi
猴 子：monkey

chēng hào chēng
称 = 号　称：claim to be

dà
大：big

wáng
王：king

chēng dà wáng
称　大　王：claim to be king; here means is king

hóu zi chēng dà wáng
猴子 称　大　王：the monkey is king

大王：对国王或首领的称呼。比喻一个地方没有杰出人物领头时，平庸之辈就出来称王称霸了。

shān gāo huáng dì yuǎn
山高皇帝远。

Proverb: The mountains are high, and the emperor is far away.
Comment: This saying was used in ancient China to describe the freedom that the provinces had as a result of poor communications, difficult terrain, and so on. The emperor was not able to control them that closely.

shān
山：mountain

gāo
高：tall

shān gāo
山 高：the mountains are high

huáng dì
皇 帝：emperor

yuǎn
远：far away

huáng dì yuǎn
皇 帝 远：the emperor is far away

shān gāo huáng dì yuǎn
山 高 皇 帝 远：the mountains are high; the emperor is far away

原指僻远的地方，中央政府的权力难以达到，现泛指离开领导机关远，这样遇事可以自作主张，不受约束，能够为所欲为。

shàn yǒng zhě nì shàn qí zhě duò
善 泳 者 溺， 善 骑 者 堕。

Proverb: The mountains are high, and the emperor is far away.
Comment: This saying was used in ancient China to describe the freedom that the provinces had as a result of poor communications, difficult terrain, and so on. The emperor was not able to control them that closely.

shàn shàn yú
善 = 善 于：be good at

yǒng yóu yǒng
泳 = 游 泳：swimming

zhě
者：a person

shàn yǒng zhě
善 泳 者：people good at swimming

nì nì shuǐ
溺 = 溺 水：drown

shàn yǒng zhě nì
善 泳 者 溺：people good at swimming will drown

qí
骑：ride

shàn qí zhě
善 骑 者：people good at horseback riding

duò shuāi xià lái
堕 = 摔 下 来：fall

shàn qí zhě duò
善 骑 者 堕：people good at horseback riding will fall

溺：淹死。堕：摔下来。善于游泳的人，往往会淹死。精于骑术的人常会摔下马来。比喻擅长某种本领的人常因疏忽大意而招致灾祸。

shàng zéi chuán róng yì xià zéi chuán nán
上 贼 船 容 易，下 贼 船 难。

Proverb: Getting on a pirate's boat is easy; getting off is hard.

Comment: Being involved with a bad person is easy, but getting rid of him is difficult. To give up evil and return to good is difficult.

shàng
上：above, get on

zéi
贼：thief

chuán
船：ship

shàng zéi chuán
上 贼 船：get on a pirate ship

róng yì
容 易：easy

xià
下：get off

xià zéi chuán
下 贼 船：get off a pirate ship

nán
难：difficult, hard

shàng zéi chuán róng yì xià zéi chuán nán
上 贼 船 容 易 下 贼 船 难：getting on a pirate's boat is easy; getting off is hard

比喻和坏人一起干坏事容易，弃邪归正却很难。

shāo xiāng dē gǎn chū hé shàng
烧 香 的 赶 出 和 尚。

Proverb: People who come to the temple burn joss sticks and drive the monks away.
Comment: Guests drive the owner away.

shāo
烧：burn

xiāng
香：joss sticks

shāo xiāng
烧 香：burn joss sticks

dē
的：'s

shāo xiāng dē
烧 香 的：the people who burn joss sticks

gǎn
赶：drive, throw out

chū
出：exit

gǎn chū
赶 出：drive away

hé shàng
和 尚：a Buddhist monk

shāo xiāng dē gǎn chū hé shàng
烧 香 的 赶 出 和 尚：people who come to the temple burn joss sticks and drive the monks away

比喻外来的人进门，反而把原来的主人赶跑了，有反客为主的意思。

shào nián fū qī lǎo lái bàn
少 年 夫 妻 老 来 伴。

Proverb: When a husband and wife are young, life is all passion; when they get older, it is companionship.
Comment: True in traditional China, true today.

shào nián
少 年：teen age

fū
夫：husband

qī
妻：wife

fū qī
夫 妻：a married couple

shào nián fū qī
少 年 夫 妻：they were a married couple when they were young

lǎo
老：old

lái
来：come

lǎo lái
老 来：getting older

bàn bàn lǚ
伴 = 伴 侣：companionionship

lǎo lái bàn
老 来 伴：when they get older, it is companionionship

年轻时结成的夫妻，到老年时就成为互相扶持的伴侣。

shēng mǐ zhǔ chéng le shóu fàn
生 米 煮 成 了 熟 饭。

Proverb: When rice has been cooked, it's too late to change it back to uncooked rice.

Comment: What's done is done. Too late to be changed. Most of the time this saying is used to talk about a man having sex or, after sex, having a child. Then a man is forced to get married.

shēng
生：uncooked

mǐ
米：rice

zhǔ
煮：cook

chéng
成：become

le
了：no meaning, used after a verb to show change already finished.

shóu
熟：cooked

fàn
饭：boiled or steamed rice

shóu fàn
熟 饭：boiled or steamed rice

zhǔ chéng lē shóu fàn
煮 成 了 熟 饭：rice has been cooked

比喻事情已成定局，无法改变。多用在婚姻方面，表示既成事实，无可奈何。

sheng nan shi long zhang zhi xi sheng nü shi long wa zhi xi
生男是弄璋之喜，生女是弄瓦之喜。

Proverb: Having a boy is like the joy of playing with jade; having a girl is like the joy of playing with a roof tile.

Comment: In ancient China, when a son was born, he was allowed to sleep on the bed, and he was given a jade article to play with. When a daughter was born, she had to sleep on the ground. She was given a roof tile to play with. It reflects the preference for boys over girls in traditional Chinese culture.

shēng shēng yù
生 = 生育：give birth to

nán
男：man, male

shēng nán
生男：give birth to a son

shì
是：is

zhāng
璋：a jade article

lòng zhāng
弄璋：play a jade article

zhī
之：'s

xǐ xǐ shì
喜 = 喜事：joyous occasion

shēng nán shì lòng zhāng zhī xǐ
生男是弄璋之喜：having a boy is like the joy of playing with jade

nǚ
女：women, female

shēng nǚ
生女：give birth to a daughter

wǎ
瓦：roof tile

lòng wǎ
弄瓦：give birth to a daughter

shēng nǚ shì lòng wǎ zhī xǐ
生女是弄瓦之喜：having a girl is like the joy of playing with a roof tile

从周代开始，生儿子就让他睡在床上，给他玩一块半圆形的玉器。生女儿，就让她睡在地下，给她玩一只陶做的纺锤。生儿或生女分别称为弄璋之喜和弄瓦之喜。虽同是喜，因为重男轻女，分量大不一样。

shèng xǐ zhōng bù xǔ rén wù shèng nù zhāng bù dā rén jiǎn
盛 喜 中 不许人物，盛 怒 中 不答人 简。

Proverb: If you are in an extremely happy mood, don't promise people gifts; if you are in an extremely angry mood, don't reply to people's letters.
Comment: Don't do or say things when you are in an unstable mood.

shèng
盛：extreme

xǐ
喜：happy

zhōng
中：in the middle of

bù
不：no, not

xǔ xǔ nuò
许 = 许 诺：make a promise

rén
人：people, a person

wù lǐ wù
物 = 礼 物：gift

shèng xǐ zhōng bù xǔ rén wù
盛 喜 中 不 许 人 物：if you are in an extremely happy mood, don't promise people gifts

nù
怒：angry

shèng nù
盛 怒：extremely angry

dá dá fù
答 = 答 复：reply

jiǎn shū jiǎn
简 = 书 简：letters

shèng nù zhōng bù dā rén jiǎn
盛 怒 中 不 答 人 简：don't reply letters when extremely angry

在大喜时不要随便许愿，在大怒时不要随意答复。指在情绪波动大的情况下，最好不要草率做出决定，以免反悔。

shī wéi jiǔ yǒu jiǔ shì sè méi
诗 为 酒 友，酒 是 色 媒。

Proverb: Poems make drunkards friends; wine is the aphrodisiac for sex.
Comment: In ancient China, intellectuals or the literati were on the top of the Confucian social order. The literati would get together, drink rice wine, recite their poems, and then, influenced by the wine, go to a brothel.

shī
诗：poems; here means write or recite poems

wéi
为：become

jiǔ
酒：wine

yǒu péng yǒu
友 = 朋 友：friend

jiǔ yǒu
酒 友：friends of drinking wine together

shī wéi jiǔ yǒu
诗 为 酒 友：poems make drunkards to be friends

shì
是：is

sè
色：color; here means sex

méi méi jiè
媒 = 媒 介：media; here means an aphrodisiac

jiǔ shì sè méi
酒 是 色 媒：wine is the aphrodisiac for sex

诗是酒的朋友，作诗能助酒兴。酒是色的媒介，酗酒能导致淫乱。

shí nián xiū dé tóng chuán dù   bǎi nián xiū dé gòng zhěn mián
十年修得同船渡，百年修得共枕眠。

Proverb: If they pray for ten years, then in their next life, two persons can cross the river in the same boat; pray one hundred years, and in their next life, two persons can be married and share a pillow to sleep.
Comment: You should treasure your relationships with others in this life.

shí
十：ten

nián
年：year

xiū   xiū xíng
修 = 修 行：pray, practice a religion

dé
得：get

tóng   gòng tóng
同 = 共 同：share

chuán
船：boat

dù
渡：cross a riverr

shí nián xiū dé tóng chuán dù
十年修得同船渡：pray for ten years and in their next life two persons can cross the river in the same boat

bǎi
百：hundred

bǎi nián
百 年：hundred years

gòng   gòng tóng
共 = 共 同：share

zhěn   zhěn tóu
枕 = 枕 头：pillow

mián
眠：sleep

gòng zhěn mián
共 枕 眠：share a pillow to sleep

bǎi nián xiū dé gòng zhěn mián
百年修得共枕眠：pray one hundred years and in their next life two persons can be married and share a pillow to sleep

比喻什么都是靠缘分，能在一起共事已属不易了，能成为夫妻，更是百年难得。用来提醒人们要珍视与人现有的关系。

shí dé jī máo dāng lìng jiàn
拾得鸡毛当令箭。

Proverb: Pick up a chicken feather and treat it as an army commander's arrow.

Comment: In ancient times, the army used a feather as a command. This proverb is said as an insult, about somebody who makes small things into a big deal.

shí dé
拾 得：pick up something

jī
鸡：chicken

máo
毛：hair, feather

jī máo
鸡 毛：chicken feather

shí dé jī máo
拾 得 鸡 毛：pick up a chicken feather

dàng dàng zuò
当 = 当 作：treat as

lìng mìng lìng
令 = 命 令：an order, a command

jiàn
箭：an arrow

lìng jiàn
令 箭：an arrow-shaped token of authority used in the army in ancient China

dāng lìng jiàn
当 令 箭：treat it as an army commander's arrow

令箭：古时军中下达命令的凭证，状似箭。比喻玩弄权术，以假充真，公然发号施令。也比喻某些人借用权威人士的只言片语去发号施令，抓小题目做大文章。

shì kě shā bù kě rǔ

士可杀，不可辱。

Proverb: You can kill intellectuals, but you cannot insult them.

Comment: In the Confucian tradition, true intellectuals live by high moral principles and would rather give up their lives than their principles.

shì shì dà fū

士 = 士大夫：man, intellectuals in ancient times

kě kě yǐ

可 = 可以：can

shā

杀：kill

shì kě shā

士可杀：can kill intellectuals

bù

不：no, not

bù kě

不可：can not

rǔ wǔ rǔ

辱 = 侮辱：insult, humiliate

bù kě rǔ

不可辱：cannot insult them

是有骨气的人表白自己的话，表示宁愿付出生命，也不愿受到别人的侮辱。

世上无不散的宴席

shì shàng wú bú sàn dē yàn xí
世上无不散的筵席。

Proverb: In this world if there is no feast, people will not leave.

Comment: If people have the time to get together, then they will feel content and leave.

shì = shì jiè
世 = 世界：world

shàng
上：above, on the top of

shì shàng
世上：in the world

wú = méi yǒu
无 = 没有：without, not have

bú
不：no, not

sàn
散：be over, leave

dē
的：'s

bú sàn dē
不散的：not leave

yàn xí
筵席：feast, banquet, party

shì shàng wú bú sàn dē yàn xí
世上无不散的筵席：in this world if there is no feast, people will not leave

筵席：酒席。指再好的聚会也有散场的时候，指有聚就必有散。

shì hòu Zhū Gé Liàng
事 后 诸 葛 亮。

Proverb: Zhu Ge Liang's wisdom came after things happened.

Comment: Zhu Ge Liang was famous for his wisdom and strategy. He could predict the result before things happened. This saying is an insult. People use it to make fun of someone who believes himself as wise as Zhu Ge Liang but who in fact is just a fake Zhu Ge Liang.

shì shì qíng
事 = 事 情：things

hòu yǐ hòu
后 = 以 后：after

shì hòu
事 后：after things happened

Zhū Gé
诸 葛：family name

Liàng
亮：first name

Zhū Gé Liàng
诸 葛 亮：a wise politician in Chinese history

shì hòu Zhū Gé Liàng
事 后 诸 葛 亮：Zhu Ge Liang's wisedom came after things happened

诸葛亮：三国时代足智多谋的政治家。讽刺人的话，指事情过后才出主意、提建议，目的是用来抬高自己。

shì	zǐ	jiǎn	ruǎn	dē	niē
柿	子	拣	软	的	捏。

Proverb: Choose the soft persimmon to squeeze.

Comment: Human nature is to bully the weak and fear the strong. Choose soft people to squeeze and give them a hard time.

shì zi
柿 子：persimmon

jiǎn
拣：pick, choose

ruǎn
软：soft

dē
的：'s

ruǎn dē
软 的：soft's; here means a weak or feeble person

niē
捏：sqeeze

shì zi jiǎn ruǎn dē niē
柿 子 拣 软 的 捏：choose the soft persimmon to squeeze

人的本性是欺软怕硬，比喻专拣软弱的人欺负。

shòu rén yǐ yú bù rú shòu rén yǐ yú
授人以鱼，不如授人以渔。

Proverb: Rather teach the person how to fish than just confer him the fish.
Comment: Give someone a fish and you feed him for a day; teach someone to fish and you feed him for a lifetime.

shòu
授：give, teach; here means give

rén
人：a person, people

shòu rén
授 人：confer a person

yǐ
以：by, with

yú
鱼：fish

shòu rén yǐ yú
授 人 以 鱼：confer a person the fish

bù
不：no, not

rú
如：as

bù rú
不 如：not as good as, rather

shòu
授：teach, give; here means teach

shòu rén
授 人：teach a person

yú
渔：fishing

bù rú shòu rén yǐ yú
不 如 授 人 以 渔：rather teach the person how to fish

授：给予。渔：捕鱼。把鱼送给人，还不如把捕鱼的方法告诉他。
比喻与其用钱财帮助人，不如教会他谋生的本领。

shòu sǐ dē luò tuó bǐ mǎ dà
瘦 死 的 骆 驼 比 马 大。

Proverb: The camel died because it was too skinny, but it was still bigger than a horse.
Comment: Even when the rich and influential lose power, they still have better lives and more influence than ordinary people.

shòu
瘦：thin

sǐ
死：die

dē
的：'s

shòu sǐ dē
瘦 死 的：died because it was too skinny

luò tuó
骆 驼：camel

shòu sǐ dē luò tuó
瘦 死 的 骆 驼：the camel died because it was too skinny

bǐ
比：compare

mǎ
马：horse

dà
大：big

bǐ mǎ dà
比 马 大：bigger then a horse

shòu sǐ dē luò tuó bǐ mǎ dà
瘦 死 的 骆 驼 比 马 大：the camel died because it was too skinny, but it was still bigger than a horse

骆驼即使是瘦饿而死，个头也比马大。比喻有钱有势的人就算是失了，也比一般人过得好；也比喻有能耐的人即使受到挫折，也比普通人强，别小看了他。

shū zhōng zì yǒu huáng jīn wū
书　中　自　有　黄　金　屋，

shū zhōng zì yǒu qiān zhōng sù
书　中　自　有　千　钟　粟，

shū zhōng zì yǒu yán rú yù
书　中　自　有　颜　如　玉。

Proverb: There is a golden house in books; there is a high salary in books; there is a beautiful woman in books.

Comment: Fame, wealth, and honor come from studying books. This is what Chinese parents say to their children.

shū
书：book

zhōng
中：in, inside, center

shū zhōng
书　中：in the book

zì　zì rán
自 = 自　然：nature

yǒu
有：have

huàng jǐn
黄　金：gold

wū
屋：house

huáng jīn wū
黄　金　屋：golden house; here means gorgeous house

shū zhōng zì yǒu huáng jīn wū
书 中 自 有 黄 金 屋：there is a golden house in books

qiān
千：thousand

zhōng
钟：gauge, a cup without handle

qiān zhōng
千 钟：thousand cups, here means a lot

sù
粟：millet, far back in history, official salary paid by millet

qiān zhōng sù
千 钟 粟：thousand cups of millet; here means highsalary

shū zhōng zì yǒu qiān zhōng sù
书 中 自 有 千 钟 粟：there is a high salary in books

yán yán miàn
颜 = 颜 面：face

rú xiàng
如 = 像：like, as

yù
玉：jade

yán rú yù
颜 如 玉：face as jade; here means very beautiful woman

shū zhī zì yǒu yán rú yù
书 中 自 有 颜 如 玉：there is a beautiful woman in books

黄金屋：指非常富丽的堂屋。千钟粟：指非常优厚的官俸。颜如玉：指非常美貌的女子。指读书人只要刻苦攻读，一切功名富贵都可从书里获得。这是用作鼓励孩子读书的座右铭。

shù dǎo hú sūn sàn
树 倒 猢 狲 散。

Proverb: When the tree falls, the monkeys on the tree scatter.
Comment: Once a powerful character falls from power, people attached to him will all scatter.

shù
树：three

dǎo
倒：collapse, fall

hú sūn
猢 狲：monkey

sàn
散：scatter

shù dǎo hú sūn sàn
树 倒 猢 狲 散：when the tree falls, the monkeys on the tree scatter

比喻作为靠山的当权人物一旦垮台，依附他的人就纷纷离散。

shù gāo qiān zhàng yè luò guī gēn
树 高 千 丈，叶 落 归 根。

Proverb: No matter how tall the tree, its leaves will fall around its roots.
Comment: This explains that people who are living far from home will come back to their hometown eventually.

shù
树：tree

gāo
高：tall, high

qiān
千：thousand

zhàng
丈：a unit of length equal 3 and 1/3 meters

qiān zhàng
千 丈：thousand zhang, use it to describing a very tall tree

shù gāo qiān zhàng
树 高 千 丈：a tree is very tall

yè
叶：leaf

luò
落：fall, drop

guī
归：come back to

gēn
根：roots

yè luò guī gēn
叶 落 归 根：its leaves will fall around its roots

秋天树叶凋落，总会落在树根周围。多用以说明长期客居他乡的人到年老时最终都要回归故里。

shuǐ qiǎn yǎng bú zhù dà yú
水 浅 养 不 住 大 鱼。

Proverb: A big fish cannot grow up in shallow water.
Comment: A small place cannot hold a "big shot." People say this when they request to be transferred to another job.

shuǐ
水：water

qiǎn
浅：shallow

yǎng
养：raise

bú
不：no, not

zhù
住：live, stop, hold

yǎng bú zhù
养不住：can't grow up

dà
大：big

yú
鱼：fish

shuǐ qiǎn yǎng bú zhù dà yú
水浅养不住大鱼：a big fish cannot grow up in shallow water

比喻小地方容不下大人物。多用在有人要求工作调走时说。

shuǐ zhì qīng zé wú yú rén zhì chá zé wú tú
水至清则无鱼，人至察则无徒。

Proverb: If the water is too clean, there are no fish; nobody will deal with people who nitpick on details.
Comment: If people are too clever and make excessive demands on others, they will have no friends or partners.

shuǐ
水：water

zhì zhì jí
至 = 至 极：extreme

qīng
清：pure, clear

shuǐ zhì qīng
水 至 清：if the water is too clean

zé
则：then

wú
无：no

yú
鱼：fish

zé wú yú
则 无 鱼：then there are no fish

rén
人：people

chá kě chá
察 = 察 觉：perceive

rén zhì chá
人 至 察：people who nitpick on details

wú méi yǒu
无 = 没 有：not have

tú
徒：people, a friend or a partner

zé wú tú
则 无 徒：then nobody will deal with him

徒：同类或伙伴的意思。水过于清澈，鱼难以生存。人太精明且过分苛察，就容不得他人过错或性格上的差异，就没有共事的伙伴和朋友。

shùn wǒ zhě chāng nì wǒ zhě wáng
顺 我 者 昌，逆 我 者 亡。

Proverb: The people who obey me will be prosperous; the people who disobey will be executed.
Comment: People say this to describe a dictator.

shùn shùn cóng
顺 = 顺 从：obedient

wǒ
我：I, me

zhě
者：a person

shùn wǒ zhě
顺 我 者：the people who obey me

chāng chāng shèng
昌 = 昌 盛：prosperous

shùn wǒ zhě chāng
顺 我 者 昌：the people who obey me will be prosperous

nì wǔ nì
逆 = 忤 逆：go against, disobey

nì wǒ zhě
逆 我 者：the people who disobey me

wáng miè wáng
亡 = 灭 亡：will be executed

nì wǒ zhě wáng
逆 我 者 亡：the people who disobey will be executed

指某些容不得不同意见的人，顺从我的就可以存在和发展，违抗我的就叫你灭亡。形容有权势的人横行霸道的行为。

shuō huà tīng shēng luó gǔ tīng yīn
说 话 听 声，锣 鼓 听 音。

Proverb: Listen to people talk, listen to their tones; listen to the gongs and drums, listen to their tempo.

Comment: People's voices can tell what mood they are in. In Chinese opera, the tempo will foretell a great event about to happen.

shuō huà
说 话：talk, speak

tīng
听：listen

shēng shēng yīn
声 = 声 音：sound, voice; here means the tones

shuō huà tīng shēn
说 话 听 声：listen to people talk, listen to their tones

luó gǔ
锣 鼓：gongs and drums

yīn shēng yīn
音 = 声 音：sound, voice; here means the tempo

luó gǔ tīng yīn
锣 鼓 听 音：listen to the gongs and drums, listen to their tempo

要想知道一个人的心情如何，听他讲话的声调，就能猜得出来，
就像京剧中的锣鼓点子声音紧了，就是有大事了。

The swastika is an ancient Buddhist symbol associated with good fortune and happiness and is frequently found on Buddhist statuary. The Nazis expropriated and reversed this symbol. In Asia the traditional swastika has no connection with Hitler or Nazism and precedes both by thousands of years.

sòng fó sòng dào xī tiān
送 佛 送 到 西 天。

Proverb: If you send Buddha to West Heaven, you must accompany him until he arrives.
Comment: West Heaven is the way Chinese refer to Buddha's birthplace. Buddha is thought to have been born in what is today south Nepal.
If you want help people, you must help them completely.

sòng
送：send somebody off

fó
佛：the deity of Buddhism

dào
到：arrive

sòng dào
送 到：send somebody until they arrive

xī
西：west

tiān
天：sky

xī tiān
西 天：ancient India, a birthplace of Buddism, west heaven

sòng fó sòng dào xī tiān
送 佛 送 到 西 天：if you send Buddha to ancient India, you must accompany him until he arrives

西天：极乐世界，佛经中指阿弥陀佛所居住的地方，佛教徒认为居住在这个地方，就可获得光明、清静和快乐，摆脱人间一切烦恼。指佛教取经的终点站。比喻帮人要帮到底，好事要做到头。

sǐ le zhāng tú fū bù chī hún máo zhū
死了张屠夫，不吃浑毛猪。

Proverb: Zhang the butcher is dead; we still don't eat the pig with hair.
Comment: Zhang butchers and cleans the hair off the pigs. Even when he dies, the pigs will still get to market without hair. Somebody will take his place. Nobody is indispensable.

sǐ le
死：die 了：no meaning, used after a verv to show change already finished

zhāng
张：family name

tú fū
屠夫：a butcher

zhāng tú fū
张屠夫：a butcher is named Zhang

sǐ le zhāng tú fū
死了张屠夫：butcher Zhang is dead

bù
不：no, not

chī
吃：eat

hún hún shēn
浑 = 浑身：all over

máo
毛：hair

zhū
猪：pig

hún máo zhū
浑毛猪：pig with hair

bù chī hún máo zhū
不吃浑毛猪：don't eat the pig with hair

张屠夫：姓张的以宰杀牲畜为职业的人。浑毛猪：没有去毛的猪肉。
比喻即使缺少了某个重要人物，事情照样能办好。

sǐ mǎ dāng zuò huó mǎ yī
死 马 当 作 活 马 医。

Proverb: Medical treatment for a dead horse as if it were a live horse.
Comment: This phrase is used when there's no hope but a person is desperate to do something anyway.

sǐ
死：die

mǎ
马：horse

sǐ mǎ
死 马：a dead horse

dāng zuò
当 作：take as

huó
活：living, alive

huó mǎ
活 马：alive horse

yī
医：treat medically

sǐ mǎ dāng zuò huó mǎ yī
死 马 当 作 活 马 医：medical treatment for a dead horse as if it were a live horse

把死马当做活马来医治。指即使到了绝望的地步，也要做最后的努力。

sǐ	zhū	bú	pà	kāi	shuǐ	tàng
死	猪	不	怕	开	水	烫。

Proverb: A dead pig is not afraid of being scalded by boiling water.
Comment: This is an insult. A person in a hopeless situation might as well risk everything. He will not mind being criticized and punished.

sǐ
死：die

zhū
猪：pig

sǐ zhū
死 猪：a dead pig

bú
不：no, not

pà
怕：afraid

shuǐ
水：water

kāi shuǐ
开 水：boiling water

tàng
烫：scald

sǐ zhū bú pà kāi shuǐ tàng
死猪不怕开水烫：a dead pig is not afraid of being scalded by boiling water

比喻人反正已经身处绝境，索性豁出去，任凭事态发展或是不在乎批评、惩罚。

táng bì dǎng chē bù zì liàng lì
蝗 臂 挡 车，不 自 量 力。

Proverb: A mantis tried to stop a cart; he overestimated his physical strength.

Comment: This means to overestimate one's ability relative to a given task.

táng táng láng
螳 = 螳 螂：a mantis

bì shǒu bì
臂 = 手 臂：an arm

dǎng zǔ dǎng
挡 = 阻 挡：stop

chē
车：a cart

táng bì dǎng chē
螳 臂 挡 车：a mantis tried to stop a cart

bù
不：no, not

zì zì jǐ
自 = 自 己：self

liàng gū liàng
量 = 估 量：estimate

lì lì liàng
力 = 力 量：physical strength

bù zì liàng lì
不 自 量 力：overestimated his physical strength

量：估量。螳臂：螳螂的前腿。指过高地估计自己的实力，强做办不到的事情。

孙猴子跳不出如来佛的掌心

sūn hóu zi tiào bù chū rú lái fó dē zhǎng xīn
孙猴子跳不出如来佛的掌心。

Proverb: The Monkey Sun cannot jump out of Ru Lain Buddha's palm.
Comment: The Monkey Sun and Ru Lain Buddha are characters in a traditional Chinese story. Monkey Sun is the king of the monkeys. No matter how great you are, you may be under control of a greater power.

sūn hóu zi
孙猴子：Monkey Sun is the King of the monkeys in children's story

tiào
跳：jump

bù
不：no, not

chū
出：exit

tiào bù chū
跳不出：can not jump out

fó
佛：the deity of Buddhism

rú lái
如来：name

rú lái fó
如来佛：Ru Lai Buddha

dē
的：'s

zhǎng shǒu zhǎng
掌 = 手掌：palm of hand

xīn zhōng xīn
心 = 中心：center

zhǎng xīn
掌心：the center of the palm

tiào bù chū rú lái fó dē zhǎng xīn
跳不出如来佛的掌心：Monkey Sun cannot jump out of Ru Lain Buddha's palm

"西游记"中的孙悟空一个跟斗能翻十万八千里，但却翻不出如来佛的手掌。借指不管如何有能耐，也摆脱不了某种力量的控制。

táng láng bǔ chán huáng què zài hòu
螳 螂 捕 蝉，黄 雀 在 后。

Proverb: A mantis is catching a cicada, but a finch is hunting right behind the mantis.
Comment: This is a warning. Don't be so eager to get something that you forget about bigger dangers that may be surrounding you.

táng láng
螳 螂：a mantis

bǔ　bǔ zhuō
捕 = 捕 捉：catch

chán
蝉：cicada

táng láng bǔ chán
螳 螂 捕 蝉：a mantis trying to hunt down a cicadas

huáng què
黄 雀：a siskin, a finch

zài
在：present, exist

hòu　hòu miàn
后 = 后 面：at the back

huáng què zài hòu
黄 雀 在 后：a finch is hunting right behind the mantis

螳螂只顾捕捉蝉，却不防黄雀在身后正要啄食自己。比喻贪图眼前利益，不顾身后祸患。

tiān lěng lěng zài fēng rén qióng qióng zài zhài

天 冷 冷 在 风，人 穷 穷 在 债。

Proverb: When the winter wind blows, it is even colder; when people are in debt, they are even poorer.

Comment: Too much debt apparently was an ancient Chinese problem as it is for Americans today.

tiān tiān qì
天 = 天 气：weather

lěng
冷：cold

tiān lěng
天 冷：weather is cold

zài
在：in

fēng
风：wind

lěng zài fēng
冷 在 风：cold in the wind

tiān lěng lěng zài fēng
天 冷 冷 在 风：when the winter wind blows, it is even colder

rén
人：people

qióng
穷：poor

zài
债：debt

qióng zài zhài
穷 在 债：poor because of be in debt

rén qióng qióng zài zhài
人 穷 穷 在 债：when people are in debt they are even poorer

指冬天怕刮风，一刮风就更寒冷，人是由于欠债才会更穷。

太太死了压断街
老爷死了没人抬
佛光
南無本師釋迦牟尼佛
南無本師釋迦牟尼佛

tài tài sǐ le yā duàn jiē lǎo yé sǐ le méi rén tái
太太死了压断街，老爷死了没人抬。

Proverb: When the wife died, her funeral procession blocked the street's traffic; when her husband died, nobody carried the coffin.
Comment: The rich and powerful husband was the one with the power. Once he died, the power was gone.

tài tài
太 太：wife

sǐ
死：died

lē
了：no meaning, used after a verb to show change already finished

tài tài sǐ le
太 太 死 了：wife died

yā
压：press down

duàn
断：cut off

jiē
街：street

yā duàn jiē
压 断 街：blocked the street's traffic

lǎo yé
老 爷：husband

méi méi yǒu
没 = 没 有：no, not

rén
人：people, a person

tái
抬：carry

lǎo yé sǐ le méi rén tái
老 爷 死 了 没 人 抬：when her husband died, nobody carried the coffin

太太去世了老爷的权势还在，巴结的人很多，都来送葬；而老爷去世了，没有了权势，连棺材也没有人抬。指世态炎凉，人情势利。

tiān shàng diào xiàn bǐng
天上掉馅饼。

Proverb: A meat pie drops from the sky.

Comment: This refers to something that is really impossible. It is used to laugh at someone who has a ridiculous idea.

tiān
天：sky

shàng
上：above, on top of

tiān shàng
天 上：on the sky

diào
掉：drop

xiàn
馅：filling

bǐng
饼：cake, biscuits

xiàn bǐng
馅 饼：a pie; here means a meat pie

tiān shàng diào xiàn bǐng
天 上 掉 馅 饼：a meat pie drops from the sky

比喻人不可能平白无故地得到好处。

tóng pén pèng le tiě sào zhou è rén zì yǒu è rén mó
铜 盆 碰 了 铁 扫 帚，恶 人 自 有 恶 人 磨。

Proverb: A copper pot hits an iron broom; evil people naturally will have evil people to torture them.

Comment: Evil people will attract even more evil people to torture them. Bad people eventually will be punished.

tóng
铜：copper

pén
盆：pot

pèng
碰：hit

le
了：no meaning, used after a verb to show change already finished

tiě
铁：iron

sào zhou
扫 帚：broom

tóng pén pèng le tiě sào zhou
铜 盆 碰 了 铁 扫 帚：a copper pot hit an iron broom

è
恶：evil

rén
人：people

è rén
恶 人：evil people

zì   zì rán
自 = 自 然：natural

yǒu
有：have

mó   zhé mó
磨 = 折 磨：torture

è rén zì yǒu è rén mó
恶 人 自 有 恶 人 磨：evil people naturally will have evil people to torture them

磨：整治。铜盆是铜做的，铁扫帚是铁做的，它们是硬碰硬。指凶恶的人，自有比他更凶恶的人对付他。也指恶人终遭恶报。

tōu jī bù zháo shí bǎ mǐ
偷 鸡 不 着 蚀 把 米。

Proverb: Failed to steal the chicken, instead lost the rice in his hand.
Comment: This phrase is used to laugh at greedy failure. The idea was to use the rice to trick the chicken and then steal it. Unfortunately, he didn't get the chicken but lost the rice.

tōu
偷：steal

jī
鸡：chicken

tōu bù zháo
偷 不 着：failed to steal

tōu jī bù zháo
偷 鸡 不 着：failed to steal the chicken

shí shí běn
蚀 = 蚀 本：lose money or things in business

bǎ
把：a measure word for handful

mǐ
米：rice

shí bǎ mǐ
蚀 把 米：lost the rice in his hand

蚀：损失。想偷鸡没偷到，反而损失一把喂鸡的米。比喻想占便宜却吃了亏。多用来劝人不要干贪便宜而没有把握的事，也嘲笑人想捞好处却受了损失。

tù zi bù chī wō biān cǎo
兔 子 不 吃 窝 边 草。

Proverb: The rabbit does not eat the grass by the side of the nest.
Comment: The grass by the side of the nest can cover the nest and can therefore protect against danger. Bad people will not do bad things around the place they are living.

tù zi
兔 子：rabbit

bù
不：not

chī
吃：eat

wō
窝：a nest

biān páng biān
边 = 旁 边：by the side of

cǎo
草：grass

wō biān cǎo
窝 边 草：the grass by the side of the nest

tù zi bù chī wō biān cǎo
兔子不吃窝边草：the rabbit does not eat the grass by the side of the nest

窝边草：可以把洞口掩盖住，以防危险。兔子为了隐藏自己，不会吃窝附近的草。比喻坏人为了立住脚，不会在住地周围做坏事。

tuō	kù	zi	fàng	pì	duō	cǐ	yī	jǔ
脱	裤	子	放	屁，	多	此	一	举。

Proverb: Taking off your pants to release gas is one more unnecessary action.

Comment: Don't make a simple thing complicated.

tuō
脱：take off

kù zi
裤子：pants

tuō kù zi
脱裤子：take off pants

fàng pì
放屁：release the gas

tuō kù zi fàng pì
脱裤子放屁：take off pants to release gas

duō
多：more, many

cǐ
此：this, these

yī
一：one

jǔ
举：a measure word for action

yī jǔ
一举：one action

duō cǐ yī jǔ
多此一举：one more unnecessary action

比喻没有必要把简单的事情搞得那么复杂。

wāi zuǐ hé shàng niàn zhēn jīng
歪 嘴 和 尚 念 真 经。

Proverb: A monk's twisted mouth chants the real scriptures.
Comment: A person with an evil intention or low ability twists something's original Comment.

wāi
歪：lop-sided

zuǐ
嘴：mouth

wāi zuǐ
歪 嘴：lopsided mouth; here means a twisted mouth

hé shàng
和 尚：a Buddhist monk

wāi zuǐ hé shàng
歪 嘴 和 尚：a twisted mouth monk

niàn
念：chant

jīn
经：scriptures

niàn jīn
念 经：chant scriptures

zhēn
真：true, real

niàn zēn jīng
念 真 经：chant the real scriptures

比喻水平低或者存心不良，歪曲了原意。

wàn è yín wéi shǒu bǎi shàn xiào wéi xiān
万 恶 淫 为 首，百 善 孝 为 先。

Proverb: Among all the evil things, promiscuity is the first; among all the virtues, filial obedience is the first.
Comment: This is the traditional Chinese moral standard

wàn
万：ten thousand

è
恶：evil

wàn è
万 恶：among a lots of evil

yín yín luàn
淫 = 淫 乱：promiscuous

wéi chéng wéi
为 = 成 为：become

shǒu shǒu yào
首 = 首 要：first

wàn è yín wéi shǒu
万 恶 淫 为 首：among all the evil things, promiscuity is the first

bǎi
百：hundred

shàn shàn shì
善 = 善 事：good thing; here means virtue

bǎi shàn
百 善：hundred good things; here mesna among all the virtues

xiào xiào shùn
孝 = 孝 顺：filial obedience

xiān
先：first

bǎi shàn xiào wéi xiān
百 善 孝 为 先：among all the virtues, filial obedience is the first

淫：指纵欲淫乱。善：善行。指所有的坏事中，淫乱是最坏的。众多美德之中，“孝”居第一位。

wáng zi fàn fǎ yǔ shù mín tóng zuì
王子犯法，与庶民同罪。

Proverb: If a prince breaks the law, he will be punished as a common person.

Comment: In front of the law, everybody is equal.

wáng zi
王子：a prince

fàn chù fàn
犯 = 触犯：offend, break

fǎ fǎ lǜ
法 = 法律：law

fàn fǎ
犯法：break the law

wáng zi fàn fǎ
王子犯法：a prince breaks the law

yǔ
与：with

shù mín
庶民：common people

tóng xiāng tóng
同 = 相同：same

zuì
罪：crime

tóng zuì
同罪：same crime; here means in front of the law, everybody is equal

yǔ shù mín tóng zuì
与庶民同罪：he will be punished as a common person

王子：国王的儿子。庶民：老百姓。王子犯法，和老百姓一样治罪。指法律面前不论地位高低，身份贵贱，人人平等。

wéi rén bù zuò kuī xīn shì bàn yè qiāo mén xīn bù jīng
为 人 不 做 亏 心 事，半 夜 敲 门 心 不 惊。

Proverb: A person who does not do unfair things to others will not be frightened when somebody knocks on the door at midnight.

Comment: A person who does not do unfair things to others will not have enemies.

wéi
为：be

rén
人：a personn, people

bú
不：not

zuò
做：doo

kuī kuī dài
亏 = 亏 待：treat unfairly

xīn
心：heart

shì
事：thing

kuī xīn shì
亏 心 事：unfair things

bàn
半：half

yè
夜：night

bàn yè
半 夜：midnight

qiāo
敲：knock

mén
门：door

xīn
心：heart

bù
不：not

jīng jīng huāng
惊 = 惊 慌：scared, be frightened

bān yè qiāo mén xīn bù jīng
半 夜 敲 门 心 不 惊：not be frightened when somebidy knocks on the door at midnight

不干坏事就问心无愧，无所畏惧，深更半夜有人敲门也不会担惊受怕。

wén wǔ zhī dào yī zhāng yī chí
文武之道，一张一弛。

Proverb: The logic of managing the country by King Zhou Wenwang and King Zhou Wuwang is that sometimes a tight policy is used, sometimes a lenient policy.

Comment: This refers to a "good guy, bad guy" approach to governance. These kings date back to the Zhou Dynasty (1100 BC). Life today should be properly balanced between tight and lenient.

wén wén wáng
文 = 文 王：king Zhou Wenwang

wǔ wǔ wáng
武 = 武 王：king Zhou Wuwang

zhī
之：'s

dào dào lǐ
道 = 道 理：logic

yī
一：one, once, once in a while

wén wǔ zhī dào
文武之道：The logic of the King Zhou Wenwang and Zhou Wuwang

zhāng zhāng kāi gōng xián
张 = 张 开 弓 弦：open the bow string; means use a tight policy

yī zhāng
一 张：one open; here means sometimes use a tight policy

chí sōng chí gōng xián
弛 = 松 弛 弓 弦：release the bow string, means use a lenient policy

yī chí
一 弛：one relase; means sometimes use a lenient policy

宽严相结合是文王武王治理国家的方法。现用来比喻生活的松紧和工作的劳逸要合理安排。

wò tà zhī cè qǐ róng tā rén hān shuì
卧榻之侧，岂容他人酣睡。

Proverb: How could you allow other people to sleep soundly on your side of the bed ?

Comment: No one should be allowed to invade or interfere with a person's or country's interests and benefits.

wò
卧：sleep

tà
榻：narrow and low bed

wò tà
卧 榻：bed

zhī
之：'s

cè
侧：side

wò tà zhī cè
卧 榻 之 侧：on the side of the bed

qǐ
岂：how could

róng róng xǔ
容 = 容 许：allow

tā
他：he

rén
人：people

tā rén
他 人：other people

hān
酣：with ease and lively, fully

shuì
睡：sleep

hān shuì
酣 睡：sleep soundly

qǐ róng tā rén hān shuì
岂 容 他 人 酣 睡：how could allow other people sleep soundly

自己的床铺边，怎么能让别人呼呼睡大觉？比喻自己的或者国家的势力范围或利益不容许别人侵占。

wú	dí	guó	wài	huàn	zhě	guó	héng	wáng
无	敌	国	外	患	者，	国	恒	亡。

Proverb: If a country is surrounded with no enemies and trouble from outside, the country will die out.

Comment: Enemies and external trouble make a person, like a country, prepared for danger.

wú méi yǒu
无 = 没 有：not have

dí
敌：enemy

guó
国：country

dí guó
敌 国：enemy country

wài
外：outside

huàn
患：trouble

wài huàn
外 患：the trouble from outside

zhě
者：people; here means a country

wú dí guó wài huàn zhě
无 敌 国 外 患 者：if a country is surrounded with no enemies and trouble from outside

hén jīng cháng
恒 = 经 常：usually

wáng miè wáng
亡 = 灭 亡：die out

guó hén wáng
国 恒 亡：the country will die out

恒：经常。在周边有敌国的情况下才会居安思危，认真正确地治理国家，否则帝王总沉迷于犬马酒色，国家就要灭亡。人必须常有对立面来警戒自己。

无事不登三宝殿

wú shì bù dēng sān bǎo diàn
无 事 不 登 三 宝 殿。

Proverb: People never go to the San Bao temple except if they want something.
Comment: Any Chinese temple devoted to the "three treasures" is called San Bao temple. The three treasures are Buddha, Dharma, and Sangha. People who go to the temple always have some important thing to ask. When they come to visit someone's home, they call the owner's home "San Bao Temple" as they enter. They want to ask for help.

wú méi yǒu
无 = 没 有：not have

shì shì qíng
事 = 事 情：things

wú shì
无 事：no thing, no business

bù
不：no, not

dēng
登：climb up; here means call at somebody's house

wú shì bù dēng
无 事 不 登：not visit somewhere except if he wanted something

sān
三：three

bǎo
宝：treasure

diàn
殿：temple

sān bǎo diàn
三 宝 殿：temple's name

"三宝"是指佛教中的佛、法、僧。"佛"是指佛主。"法"是佛教教义。"僧"是继承、宣扬佛教教义的众和尚。"三宝殿"：三宝所在的寺庙就是三宝殿了。没事就不会到佛殿去求神拜佛。指只要登门，必是有事相求。

wú guān yī shēn qīng yǒu zǐ wàn shì zú
无官一身轻，有子万事足。

Proverb: If you are not an official, you can totally relax; if you have a son, you will be totally satisfied.

Comment: This Proverb reflects the traditional Chinese reliance on family rather than government institutions.

wú = méi yǒu
无 = 没有：not have

guān
官：official, here means official title

wú guān
无官：not to be an official

yī
一：one

shēn
身：body

yī shēn
一身：whole body

qīng = qīng sōng
轻 = 轻松：relax

wú guān yī shēn qīng
无官一身轻：if you are not an official, you can totally relax

yǒu
有：have

zǐ
子：son

wàn
万：ten thousand

shì
事：things

zú = mǎn zú
足 = 满足：satisfaction

wàn shì zú
万事足：everything satisfied; here means totally satisfied

yǒu zǐ wàn shì zú
有子万事足：if you have a son, you will be totally satisfied

没有官职一身轻松，有了子孙万事满足。原为居官的人解除公职后自我安慰之辞。形容卸去了责任，希望有了寄托的适意心情。

wú yuān bù chéng fū qī wú zhài bù chéng fù zǐ

无冤不成夫妻，无债不成父子。

Proverb: If no injustice from the last life, no need to be a married couple in this life; if no debt from the last life, no need to be father and son in this life.

Comment: Chinese believe problems get carried over from the previous life. For example, two people who fought in the last life can come back as a married couple and keep fighting. A father who owed someone in the last life comes back as his father, and in turn, his money is squandered by his son.

wú méi yǒu
无 = 没 有：not have

yuān
冤：an injustice or wrong

bù
不：things

chéng chéng wéi
成 = 成 为：become

fū
夫：husband

qī
妻：wife

wú yuān bù chéng fū qī
无 冤 不 成 夫 妻：if no injustice from the last life, no need to be a married couple in this life

zhài
债：debt

wú zhài
无 债：no debt

fù
父：father

zǐ
子：son

wú zhài bù chéng fù zǐ
无 债 不 成 夫 子：if no debt from last life, no need to be father and son in this life

中国人相信夫妻之间经常会吵吵闹闹，前世若无冤仇，今世便成不了夫妻。父亲是前世欠了债，儿子今世就是来讨债的，否则便成不了父子。

wù bì xiān fǔ ér hòu chóng shēng zhī
物必先腐而后虫生之，

rén bì zì wǔ ér hòu rén wǔ zhī
人必自侮而后人侮之。

Proverb: Things must spoil first, and then the worm will grow; a person must insult himself first, and then other people will insult him.

Comment: People should respect themselves, and then others will respect them.

wù
物：things

bì bì rán
必 = 必然：sure, must

xiān
先：first, earlier

fǔ fǔ bài
腐 = 腐败：spoil

wù bì xiān fǔ
物必先腐：things must spoil first

ér
而：a link word between two things; here means then

hòu
后：after, late

ér hòu
而后：then later

chóng
虫：a worm

shēng shēng zhǎng
生 = 生长：grow

zhī
之：it; here means the things

chóng shēng zhī
虫 生 之：the worm will grow

ér hòu chóng shēng zhī
而 后 虫 生 之：then the worm will grow

rén
人：a person, people

zì zì jǐ
自 = 自 己：self

wǔ wǔ rǔ
侮 = 侮 辱：insult, humiliate

rén bì zì wǔ
人 必 自 侮：a person must insult himself

ér hòu
而 后 ：then

zhī
之：him; here means the person himself

rén wǔ zhī
人 侮 之：other people will insult him

ér hòu rén wǔ zhī
而 后 人 侮 之：then other people will insult him

侮：侮辱，不尊重。指内部和外部的关系，人若不尊重自己，当然也得不到别人的尊重，就像东西只有自己先腐烂了，然后才会生虫，应该从内部找原因。

xǐ shí zhī yán duō shī xìn nù shí zhī yán duō shī tǐ
喜时之言多失信，怒时之言多失体。

Proverb: When people talk in a happy mood, many times they lose credit; when people talk in an angry mood, many times they lose dignity.
Comment: This proverb warns people to speak carefully when emotional.

xǐ
喜：happy

shí
时：time

xǐ shí
喜时：in a happy mood

zhī
之：'s

yán
言：talk

xǐ shí zhī yán
喜时之言：talk in a happy mood

duō
多：many

shī
失：lost

xìn xìn yòng
信 = 信用：credit

duō shī xìn
多失信：many times lose credit

nù
怒：angry

nù shí
怒时：in an angry mood

nù shí zhī yán
怒时之言：talk in an angry mood

tǐ tǐ miàn
体 = 体面：dignity

shī tǐ
失体：lose dignity

duō shī tǐ
多失体：many times lose dignity

高兴时说的话大都难以兑现，发怒时所说的话常常有失体面。告诫人在感情冲动时，出言更要慎重。

xiā māo zhuàng shàng sǐ hào zi
瞎 猫 撞 上 死 耗 子。

Proverb: A blind cat collides with a dead mouse.

Comment: To get something by unexpected good luck.

xiā
瞎：blind

māo
猫：cat

xiā māo
瞎 猫：a blind cat

zhuàng shàng
撞 上：collide with

sǐ
死：dead

hào zi
耗 子：mouse

sǐ hào zi
死 耗 子：a dead mouse

xiā māo zhuàng shàng sǐ hào zi
瞎 猫 撞 上 死 耗 子：a blind cat collides with a dead mouse

比喻侥幸得到意外的收获或成功。

xià chóng bù kě yǔ yǔ bīng
夏 虫 不 可 与 语 冰。

Proverb: You cannot discuss ice with a summer worm.

Comment: A summer worm's life is very short. It never lives in the winter. You cannot discuss something with people who have never experienced it.

xià xià tiān
夏 = 夏 天：summer

chóng
虫：worm

xià chóng
夏 虫：a summer worm

bù
不：no, not

kě kě yǐ
可 = 可 以：can

bù kě
不 可：cannot

yǔ
与：with

yǔ tán lùn
语 = 谈 论：discuss

bīng
冰：ice

xià chóng bù kě yǔ yǔ bīng
夏 虫 不可与语冰：you cannot discuss ice with a summer worm

夏天的昆虫生命短暂，没有经历过冬天的寒冷，是不可能同它谈论冬天发生的事情的。比喻和没有经历的人是谈不到一起的。

xiān xiǎo rén hòu jūn zǐ
先 小 人，后 君 子。

Proverb: First, act as a villain; then act as a gentleman.
Comment: In other words, be tough in the beginning and a gentleman later.

xiān
先：first, earlier, in advance

xiǎo
小：small

rén
人：people, a person

xiǎo rén
小 人：villain

xiān xiǎo rén
先 小 人：first act as a villain

hòu rán hòu
后 = 然 后：then, next

jūn zǐ
君 子：a gentleman

hòu jūn zǐ
后 君 子：then act as a gentleman

指办事前先把有关条件、要求等讲明谈妥，看似斤斤计较，实际上事后免除了纠纷，才能像君子一样彼此礼让三分。

xiān huā chā zài niú fèn shàng
鲜 花 插 在 牛 粪 上。

Proverb: A fresh flower stuck in cow manure.
Comment: This phrase is used to describe a beautiful woman married to a terrible man.

xiān xīn xiān
鲜 = 新 鲜：fresh

huā
花：flower

xiān huā
鲜 花：a fresh flower; here means a beautiful woman

chā
插：stuck

zài
在：in

niú
牛：cow

fèn
粪：manure

shàng
上：on top of

zài niú fèn shàng
在 牛 粪 上：on top of the cow manure

xiān huā chā zài niú fèn shàng
鲜 花 插 在 牛 粪 上：a fresh flower stuck in cow manure

比喻一个如花似玉的美女嫁给很糟糕的男人。

xián shí bù shāo xiāng jí shí bào fó jiǎo
闲 时 不 烧 香，急 时 抱 佛 脚。

Proverb: People don't burn joss sticks when they have leisure time; they clasp Buddha's feet in their arms during emergencies.

Comment: People only rush to ask for help at the last minute when they have a problem.

xián
闲：leisure

shí shí hòu
时 = 时 候：time

xián shí
闲 时：leisure time

bù
不：no, not

shāo xiāng
烧 香：burn joss sticks

xián shí bù shāo xiāng
闲 时 不 烧 香：don't burn joss sticks when they have leisure time

jí
急：emergency

shí
时：time

bào
抱：clasp

fó
佛：Buddha

jiǎo
脚：feet

bào fó jiǎo
抱 佛 脚：hold Buddha's feet in the arms

jí shí bào fó jiǎo
急 时 抱 佛 脚：hold Buddha's feet in their arms during emergencies; here means in a last-minute rush

平时不烧香，有急难才向佛求救，比喻平时不极积做准备，事到临头才急忙应付。

项庄舞剑
意在沛公

xiàng zhuāng wǔ jiàn yì zài pèi gōng
项　庄　舞 剑，意 在 沛 公。

Proverb: Xiang Zhuang dances with a double-edged straight sword; his objective is Pei Gong.

Comment: This comes from a famous Han Dynasty story of "Hong Ming Yan." Emperor Xiang Yu entertains Pei Gong with dinner at his palace. During the dinner, the emperor asks his subordinate Xiang Zhuang to dance with a double-edged straight sword to add to the fun. In fact, the emperor wants to take this opportunity to assassinate his competitor Pei Gong. Later generations use this story to indicate some people have legitimate reasons on the surface, but in fact have ulterior motives.

xiàng zhuāng
项　庄：Xiang Zhuang, Han dynasty Emporer

wǔ
舞：dance

jiàn
剑：a double-edged straight sword

wǔ jiàn
舞 剑：dance with sword

xiàng zhuāng wǔ jiàn
项　庄　舞 剑：Xiang Zhuang dances with a double-edged straight sword

yì　yì tú
意 = 意 图：purpose

zài
在：at

pèi gōng
沛 公：Pei Gong

yì zài pèi gōng
意 在 沛 公：objective is Pei Gong; here means he wants assassinate Pei Gong

项庄：项羽的手下。沛公：刘邦的尊称。出自历史故事《鸿门宴》。刘邦和项羽是历史上的两个对手。项羽宴请刘邦，让手下项庄舞剑助兴，打算趁机刺杀刘邦。后人用它来指某些人表面有正当名目，实际上却是别有用心。

xiǎng gǔ bú yòng zhòng chuí qiāo
响 鼓 不 用 重 锤 敲。

Proverb: You don't have to use a heavy hammer to beat on a loud drum.
Comment: Capable people don't have to be pressed. They always can do a good job.

xiǎng
响：loud sound

gǔ
鼓：drum

xiǎng gǔ
响 鼓：a drum can make a loud sound if you beat on it

bú
不：no, not

yòng
用：use

zhòng
重：heavy weight

chuí
锤：hammer

zhòng chuí
重 锤：a heavy hammer

qiāo
敲：beat

xiǎng gǔ bú yòng zhòng chuí qiāo
响 鼓 不 用 重 锤 敲：don't have to use a heavy hammer to beat on a loud drum

比喻能干的人，不用旁人督促，也能把事情做好。

xiǎo bù rěn zé luàn dà móu
小 不 忍 则 乱 大 谋。

Proverb: If you do not put up with little things, you will jeopardize a big strategy.

Comment: Good advice.

xiǎo
小：little, here means little things

bù
不：no, not

rěn
忍：put up with

xiǎo bù rěn
小 不 忍：not put up with little things

zé
则：then

luàn gǎo luàn
乱 = 搞 乱：jeopardize

dà
大：big

móu jì móu
谋 = 计 谋：strategy

dà móu
大 谋：a big strategy

xiǎo bù rěn zé luàn dà móu
小 不 忍 则 乱 大 谋：if you do not put up with little things, you will jeopardize a big strategy

谋：计谋。指小的地方不去忍让就会坏了大事。

xiǎo ér yù dé ān cháng dài sān fēn jī hé hán
小儿欲得安，常带三分饥和寒。

Proverb: If you want the little baby to be safe and well, keep it 30 percent hungry and cold.

Comment: Don't feed kids too much or put too much clothing on them.

xiǎo
小：small, little

ér
儿：son, baby

xiǎo ér
小儿：a little baby

yù
欲：want

dé
得：to be

ān píng ān
安 = 平安：safe and well

xiǎo ér yù dé ān
小儿欲得安：want the little baby to be safe and well

cháng
常：always

dài
带：bring

sān
三：three

fēn
分：divide into parts

sān fēn
三分：30 percent

jī jī è
饥 = 饥饿：hungry

hé
和：and

hán hán lěng
寒 = 寒冷：cold

cháng dài sān fēn jī hé hán
常带三分饥和寒：keep it 30 percent hungry and cold

小孩子想要不生病，不要让他吃得太饱，穿得太暖。

xiǎo jiǎo yī shuāng yǎn lèi yī gāng
小 脚 一 双，眼 泪 一 缸。

Proverb: One pair of small feet costs one bucket of tears.
Comment: From the Song Dyasty (960–1278) until the end of the Qing Dynasty (1644-1911), women's feet were bound. A woman was beautiful if her feet were three inches long. This binding was an extremely painful process.

xiǎo
小：small

jiǎo
脚：feet

xiǎo jiǎo
小 脚：three-inch feet

yī
一：one

shuāng
双：a pair

xiǎo jiǎo yī shuāng
小 脚 一 双：a pair of small feet

yǎn
眼：eye

lèi
泪：tears

yǎn lèi
眼 泪：tears

gāng
缸：bucket

yī gāng
一 缸：one bucket

yǎn lèi yī gāng
眼 泪 一 缸：one bucket of tears

小脚又叫三寸金莲，是用布条子把脚扎裹起来，使其变得又小又尖的一种封建陋俗，是对中国妇女精神上和肉体上的严重摧残。要裹出一双合格的小脚就要付出流满一缸眼泪的代价。

xiào	pín	bú	xiào	chāng
笑	贫	不	笑	娼。

Proverb: People ridicule the poor but not whores.

Comment: This is a negative view on society's attitudes.

xiào　jī xiào
笑 = 讥 笑：ridicule

pín　pín qióng
贫 = 贫 穷：poor

xiào pín
笑 贫：ridicule at poor

bú
不：no, not

chāng chāng jì
娼 = 娼 妓：whore

xiào chāng
笑 娼：ridicule whore

xiào pín bú xiào chāng
笑 贫 不 笑 娼：ridicule the poor, not the whore

指社会风气不好，人们不去嘲笑娼妓，而是去嘲笑穷人。

xīn guān shàng rèn sān bǎ huǒ
新 官 上 任 三 把 火。

Proverb: A new official sets a fire three times on the first day of his job.
Comment: This proverb is used to laugh at some people who are very enthusiastic in the beginning, but run out of energy later.

xīn
新：new

guān
官：an officer

xīn guān
新 官：a new officer

shàng rèn
上 任：the first day on his job

xīn guān shàng rèn
新 官 上 任：an new official on the first day of his job

sān
三：three

bǎ huǒ bǎ
把 = 火 把：torch

sān bǎ
三 把：three torches; here means set the fire three times

sān bǎ huǒ
三 把 火：set the fire three times

指刚上任的官为树立威望，总要尽心尽力地干几件好事。比喻人刚开始做事时热情很高，但未必能持久。

秀才遇到兵
有理说不清

xiù cái yù dào bīng yǒu lǐ shuō bù qīng

秀才遇到兵，有理说不清。

Proverb: A scholar runs into a soldier; even with right on his side, the scholar cannot reason with him.

Comment: Don't argue with unreasonable people. This only wastes time.

xiù cái
秀 才：a scholar, someone who passed the imperial examination at the country level in Ming and Qing dynasties

yù dào
遇 到：run into

bīng
兵：soldier

xiù cái yù dào bīng
秀 才 遇 到 兵：a scholar runs into a soldier

yǒu
有：have

lǐ dào lǐ
理 = 道 理：a reason

yǒu lǐ
有 理：in the right

shuō
说：tell, speak

bù
不：no, not

qīng qīng chǔ
清 = 清 楚：clear

yǒu lǐ suō bù qīng
有 理 说 不 清：even with right on his side, the scholar cannot reason with him

比喻讲道理的人遇到蛮横的人，即使再有道理也说不清。

xíng bú shàng dà fū lǐ bú xià shù rén
刑不上大夫，礼不下庶人。

Proverb: Corporal punishment cannot be applied to nobles; courteous treatment is not extended to the common people.
Comment: In traditional China, when crimes were committed, the law was not the same for different people. Nobles qualified for no punishment. Common people qualified for no courteous treatment.

xíng = xíng fǎ
刑 = 刑法：corporal punishment

bú
不：no, not

shàng = shàng dào
上 = 上到：up to

dà fū = guì zú
大夫 = 贵族：nobles

xíng bú shàng dà fū
刑不上大夫：corporal punishment cannot be applied to nobles

lǐ = lǐ jié
礼 = 礼节：courtesy, here means courteous treatment

xià = xià dào
下 = 下到：down to

shù rén
庶人：the common people

lǐ bú xià shù rén
礼不下庶人：courteous treatment is not extended to the common people

大夫拥有特权不受刑，庶人没有资格受礼遇。在封建社会里，法律因人论罪，尊上卑下。贵族犯了法，可以不治罪，普通百姓没有资格得到礼遇。

xīn jí chī bù liǎo rè dòu fu
心 急 吃 不 了 热 豆 腐。

Proverb: Impatient people cannot eat hot bean curd.

Comment: If impatient, you cannot achieve a goal.

xīn
心：heart

jí
急：urgent

xīn jí
心 急：impatient

chī
吃：eat

bù liǎo
不 了：without end, use it after a verb

chī bù liǎo
吃 不 了：cannot eat

xìn jí chī bù liǎo
心 急 吃 不 了：impatient cannot eat

rè
热：hot

dòu fu
豆 腐：bean curd

rè dòu fu
热 豆 腐：hot bean curd

热豆腐很烫，指性子太急，办事常达不到预期的目的。

xú niáng bàn lǎo fēng yùn yóu cún
徐 娘 半 老，风 韵 犹 存。

Proverb: Madam Xu in middle age was still very sexy.
Comment: People use Madam Xu as a metaphor to name any middle-aged woman who still is sexually attractive.

xú
徐：Xu is a family name

xú niáng
徐 娘：a woman whose family name is Xu

bàn 半：half | lǎo 老：old | bàn lǎo 半 老：middle aged

xú niáng bàn lǎo
徐 娘 半 老：madam Xu is middle aged

fēng yùn
风 韵：sexual personal charm

yóu hái
犹 = 还：still

cún cún zài
存 = 存 在：exist

fēng yùn yóu cún
风 韵 犹 存：still had sexual personal charm

徐娘：南朝梁元帝之妃徐昭佩，这里泛指中年女人。风韵：风度和韵味，指性感的魅力。人们常以"半老徐娘"来称呼年老而尚有风韵的妇女.

xuě yuán qīn　dǎ duàn gǔ tóu lián zhē jīn
血 缘 亲，打 断 骨 头 连 着 筋。

Proverb: Blood relationship is intimate; bones may snap into two, but veins still link together.
Comment: A graphic description depicting the strength of family ties in traditional Chinese society.

xuě
血：blood

yuán　yuán fèn
缘 = 缘 分：people are brought together by fate

xuě yuán
血 缘：blood relationship

qīn
亲：intimate

xuě yuán qīn
血 缘 亲：the intimate blood relationship

dǎ
打：hit

duàn
断：snap in two

gǔ tóu
骨 头：bone

dǎ duàn gǔ tóu
打 断 骨 头：hit the bone, and the bone snaps in two

lián
连：link

zhē
着：no meaning, indicate action or status is continued

jīn
筋：veins

lián zhē jīn
连 着 筋：veins linked together

dǎ duàn gǔ tóu lián zhē jīn
打 断 骨 头 连 着 筋：blood relationship is intimate; bones may snap into two, but veins still link together

有血缘关系的人，他们之间的亲情是难以割断的。

肃静
衙门朝南开
有钱无理莫进来

yá mén cháo nán kāi yǒu lǐ méi qián mò jìn lái
衙门朝南开，有理没钱莫进来。

Proverb: The court's door opens to the south; if you are in the right but don't have money, don't enter.
Comment: In traditional China, officials recognized only money, not principles. If you want to win a lawsuit, you have to bribe officials.

yá mén
衙门：court

cháo
朝：face

nán
南：south

kāi
开：open

cháo nán kāi
朝南开：opens to the south

yá mén cháo nán kāi
衙门朝南开：the court's door opens to the south

yǒu
有：have

lǐ
理：a principle

yǒu lǐ
有理：in the right

méi méi yǒu
没 = 没有：don't have

qián
钱：money

mò bú yào
莫 = 不要：do not

jìn lái
进来：enter

yǒu lǐ méi qián mò jìn lái
有理没钱莫进来：if you are in the right but don't have money, don't enter

衙门：旧时官员办公的机关。指官府认钱不认理，想打赢官司要用钱行贿。

yào xiǎng yī tiāng bù shū fu
要想一天不舒服，

chuān shuāng xiǎo xié zi
穿双小鞋子；

yào xiǎng yī bèi zi bù shū fu
要想一辈子不舒服，

yǒu liǎng gè nǚ rén
有两个女人。

Proverb: If you want to be unhappy for a day, wear a pair of shoes that are too small; if you want to be unhappy for life, have two women.
Comment: Good advice for all the world's playboys

yào yào shì
要 = 要是：if

xiǎng
想：want

yī
一：one

tiān
天：day

bù
不：no, not

shū fu
舒服：comfortable

bù shū fu
不舒服：uncomfortable, here means unhappy

yào xiǎng yī tiān bù shū fu
要想一天不舒服：want to be unhappy for a day

chuān
穿：wear

shuāng
双：a pair

xiǎo
小：small, little

xié zi
鞋 子：shoes

xiǎo xié zi
小 鞋 子：small shoes; here means the small shoes squeeze the feet

chuān shuāng xiǎo xié zi
穿 双 小 鞋 子：wear a pair of small shoes

yī bèi zi
一 辈 子：whole life

yào xiǎng yī bèi zi bù shū fu
要 想 一 辈 子 不 舒 服：if you want to be unhappy for life

yǒu
有：have

liǎng
两：two

gè
个：a measure word for counting people

nǚ rén
女人：woman

yǒu liǎng gè nǚ rén
有 两 个 女 人：have two women

小鞋子夹脚，穿上不会舒服，就像同时拥有两个女人，可以闹到终生不太平。

yán wáng hǎo jiàn xiǎo guǐ nán chán
阎 王 好 见，小 鬼 难 缠。

Proverb: It's easy to deal with the king of hell, but not with a little ghost.
Comment: Usually, servants are more difficult to deal with than the master.

yán wáng
阎 王：the king of hell

hǎo
好：good; here means easy

jiàn
见：meet

hǎo jiàn
好 见：easy to deal

yán wáng hǎo jiàn
阎 王 好 见：easy to deal with the king of hell

xiǎo
小：little

guǐ
鬼：ghost

xiǎo guǐ
小 鬼：a little ghost

nán
难：difficult, hard

chán jiū chán
缠 = 纠 缠：get entangled with

nán chán
难 缠：hard to get entangled with

xiǎo guǐ nán chán
小 鬼 难 缠：a little ghost is hard to get entangled with

为首的往往还讲点道理，手下人仗势欺人，下面的人比上面的人更难对付。

yáng ròu méi chī dào rě le yī shēn yáng sāo chòu
羊 肉 没 吃 到，惹 了 一 身 羊 膻 臭。

Proverb: Didn't eat the mutton but still stinks like sheep.

Comment: This saying refers to a situation in which someone tried to get benefits but without success. Instead he just got troubles.

yáng
羊：sheep

yáng ròu
羊 肉：mutton

méi méi yǒu
没 = 没 有：not have

chī
吃：eat

chī dào
吃 到：ate already

méi chī dào
没 吃 到：didn't eat yet

yáng ròu méi chī dào
羊 肉 没 吃 到：didn't eat the mutton

rě
惹：bring trouble

le
了：no meaning, used after a verb to show change already finished

yī
一：one

shēn
身：body

yī shēn
一 身：whole body

sāo chòu
膻 臭：stink

rě le yī shēn yáng sāo chòu
惹 了 一 身 羊 膻 臭：brings trouble, whole body stinks like a sheep

比喻好处没有得到，却招来了麻烦。

yī gè hé shàng tiāo shuǐ hē
一个和尚挑水喝，

liǎng gè hé shàng tái shuǐ hē
两个和尚抬水喝，

sān gè hé shàng méi shuǐ hē
三个和尚没水喝。

Proverb: One monk with a pole on his shoulder carries two buckets of water to drink; two monks with a pole on their shoulders carry a bucket of water to drink; three monks have no water to drink.
Comment: Too many people make responsibility unclear and cannot do a good job.

yī
一：one

gè
个：a measure word for people

hé shàng
和尚：monk

yī gè hé shàng
一个和尚：one monk

tiāo
挑：carry things with shoulder pole

shuǐ
水：water

hē
喝：drink

tiāo shuǐ hē
挑水喝：a pole on the shoulder carries two buckets of water to drink

yī gè hé shàng tiāo shuǐ hē
一个和尚挑水喝：one monk with a pole on his shoulder carries two buckets of water to drink

liǎng
两：two

liǎng gè hé shàng
两个和尚：two monks

tái
抬：raise

tái shuǐ
抬水：carry water with a pole

liǎng gè hé shàng tái shuǐ hē
两个和尚抬水喝：two monks with a pole on their shoulders carry a bucket of water to drink

sān
三：three

sān gè hé shàng
三个和尚：three monks

méi méi yǒu
没 = 没有：not have

méi shuǐ hē
没水喝：no water to drink

sān gè hé shàng méi shuǐ hē
三个和尚没水喝：three monks have no water to drink

比喻人虽少，但责任明确，事情容易办成。人多了，责任不明确，一项工作由很多人来做，就会因为自私而互相推委，反而办不好事情。

yǎng ér fáng lǎo jī gǔ fáng jī
养 儿 防 老，积 谷 防 饥。

Proverb: Raise children to provide for old age, just like saving the unhusked rice to provide against hunger.

Comment: Unhusked rice is easier to store. A person should prepare for tasks ahead.

yǎng
养：raise

ér
儿：son; here means children

fáng yù fáng
防 = 预 防：provide

lǎo lǎo nián
老 = 老 年：old age, elderly

yǎng ér fáng lǎo
养 儿 防 老：raise children to provde for old age

jī jī xù
积 = 积 蓄：save

gǔ dào gǔ
谷 = 稻 谷：unhusked rice

jī gǔ
积 谷：saving the unhusked rice; here means saving food

jī jī è
饥 = 饥 饿：hunger

fáng jī
防 饥：provide against hunger

jī gǔ fáng jī
积 谷 防 饥：saving the unhusked rice to provide against hunger

养育儿子是为了自己老年时有人赡养，积谷是预防灾荒年没饭吃，指凡事要事先做好准备，以防后患。

ye cao nan fei tai shou ma heng cai bu fu ming qiong ren
野草 难肥胎瘦 马，横 财不富命 穷 人。

Proverb: Wild grass cannot make a skinny horse fat if it was thin in the womb; money that comes suddenly cannot make a person rich whom fate has made poor.

Comment: In Chinese culture peoples lives are decided by fate.

ye
野：wild

cao
草：grass, straw

ye cao
野 草：wild grass

nan
难：no, not

fei
肥：fat

nan fei
难 肥：not fat

tai
胎：womb

shou
瘦：thin

ma
马：horse

ye cao nan fei tai shou ma
野草 难肥胎瘦 马：wild grass cannot make a skinny horse fat if it was thin in the womb

hen cai
横 财：suddenly comes money

bu
不：not

bu fu
不富：not rich

ming ming yun
命 = 命 运：fate

qiong
穷：poor

ming qiong
命 穷：a poor fate

ren
人：person

heng cai bu fu ming qiong ren
横 财不富命 穷 人：money that comes suddenly cannot make a person rich whom fate has made poor

命：宿命，命中注定的意思。胎瘦：先天不足。指先天不足的马再调养也养不肥，命中注定的穷人，即使得到了横财也富不起来。

yī gāo zi dǎ chén yī chuán rén
一 篙 子 打 沉 一 船 人。

Proverb: One stroke with the bamboo pole against the boat, and all the people on the boat sink.
Comment: Give all the people the same punishment before finding out the truth.

yī
一：one

gāo zi
篙 子：bamboo pole

yī gāo zi
一 篙 子：uas bamboo pole to strike one time

dǎ
打：strike

chén
沉：sink

chuán
船：boat

rén
人：people, a person

yī chuán rén
一 船 人：all the people on the boat

yī gāo zi dǎ chén yī chuán rén
一 篙 子 打 沉 一 船 人：one stroke with the bamboo pole against the boat, and all the people on the boat sink

撑船的一篙子打过去，将一船人全部打翻到水里。比喻某些人不搞清事实的真相，不分好坏地给所有的人同样的惩治。

yī lì lǎo shǔ shǐ huài le yī guō tāng
一粒老鼠屎，坏了一锅汤。

Proverb: One small piece of mouse shit can spoil a whole pot of soup.
Comment: If bad people or bad things sneak into a group or place, the entirety will be damaged.

yī
一：one

lì
粒：one small piece

lǎo shǔ
老鼠：mouse

shǐ
屎：shit

yī lì lǎo shǔ shǐ
一粒老鼠屎：one small piece of mouse shit

huài lòng huài
坏 = 弄坏：spoil

lē
了：no meaning, used after an adject to show change already finished

guō
锅：pot

tāng
汤：soup

yī guō tāng
一锅汤：a whole pot of soup

huài lē yī guō tāng
坏了一锅汤：spoil a whole pot of soup

比喻掺杂一个坏人或坏的东西，会使整体受到损害。

yī rén dé dào jī quǎn shēng tiān
一 人 得 道，鸡 犬 升 天。

Proverb: A person rises in power and becomes important; even his chickens and dogs will rise to the sky.
Comment: If one person rises in power, others who have ties of kinship or friendship will follow him.

yī
一：one

rén
人：people, a person

dé dào
得 道：rise in power

yī rén dé dào
一 人 得 道：one person rises in power

jī
鸡：chicken

quǎn
犬：dog

shēng
升：rise

tiān
天：sky

jī quǎn shēng tiān
鸡 犬 升 天：chickens and dogs will rise to the sky

升天：腾飞升到天上，指发迹。淮南王刘安修道成仙，他剩下的灵丹仙药鸡狗吃后也随之升天。一个人发迹，连他一家的鸡狗都成了神仙。指因一人得势，沾亲带故的人都会随之发迹。

yī wǎn mǐ yǎng gè ēn rén yī dǒu mǐ yǎng gè chóu rén
一碗米养个恩人，一斗米养个仇人。

Proverb: Give a person one bowl of rice, and you are a benefactor; give a person fifteen kilograms of rice, and you will create an enemy.
Comment: Help people only when they are having a hard time. Otherwise, they will feel entitled to your support and become your enemy. The Chinese proverb is expressed in traditional Chinese measurements, nor liters.

yī
一：one

wǎn
碗：bowl

mǐ
米：rice

yī wǎn mǐ
一碗米：one bowl of rice; here means a little rice

yǎng
养：raise

gè
个：a

ēn rén
恩人：a benefactor

yī wǎn mǐ yǎng gè ēn rén
一碗米养个恩人：give a person one bowl of rice, and you are a benefactor

dǒu
斗：a unit of dry measure for grain

yī dǒu mǐ
一斗米：fifteen kilograms of rice

chóu rén
仇人：an enemy

yī dǒu mǐ yǎng gè chóu rén
一斗米养个仇人：give a person fifteen kilograms of rice, and you will create an enemy

升是容积单位 斤是重量单位，是中国古代计量方法即：一斗为十升，每升约重1.5公斤。一碗米少，一斗米多。一个人饥寒交迫的时候，你给他一碗米，就解决了他的大问题，他会把你当恩人。但给人过分多的帮助，会养成人家对你的依赖，因不满足而成为仇人。

yī zhāo bèi shé yǎo shí nián pà jǐng shéng
一朝被蛇咬，十年怕井绳。

Proverb: Once bitten by a snake, afraid of a well rope for ten years.

Comment: Once bitten, twice shy.

yī
一：one

zhāo
朝：morning, in one dayday

yī zhāo
一朝：once

bèi
被：a word used before the main verb to express the passive

shé
蛇：snake

yǎo
咬：bite

yī zhāo bèi shé yǎo
一朝被蛇咬：once bitten by a snake

shí
十：ten

nián
年：year

shí nián
十年：ten years

pà
怕：afraid

jǐng
井：a well

shéng
绳：a rope

shí nián pà jǐng shéng
十年怕井绳：afraid of a well rope for ten years

有一天被蛇咬了，十年都会害怕，见到井绳以为又是蛇。比喻遭到一次灾难或挫折以后，心有余悸。多用来说人受到惊吓以后变得胆小怕事了。

yī rén zào fǎn zhū lián jiǔ zú
一人造反，株连九族。

Proverb: One person rebels against the government, and punishment will be visited on nine families who are relations.
Comment: In traditional China, if a person rebels against the government, everyone in the extended family is responsible and will be punished.

yī
一：one

rén
人：person

zào fǎn
造反：rebel against the government

yī rén zào fǎn
一人造反：one person rebels against the government

zhū lián
株连：implicate; here means inflict punishment

jiǔ
九：nine

zú = jiā zú
族 = 家族：extended families

jiǔ zú
九族：nine families; here means extended family

zhū lián jiǔ zú
株连九族：punishment will be visited on nine families who are relations

株连：牵连，连累。旧时把反叛朝廷定为滔天大罪，不仅本人死罪难逃，还要连累自己所有的亲族。

yī	shān	róng	bú	xià	èr	hǔ
一	山	容	不	下	二	虎。

Proverb: One mountain cannot hold two tigers.

Comment: One place cannot have two powerful persons coexisting.

yī
一：one

shāng
山：mountain

róng róng nà
容 = 容 纳：hold

bú
不：no, not

xià
下：down, under

róng bú xià
容 不 下：cannot hold

èr
二：two

hǔ
虎：tiger

yī shān róng bú xià èr hǔ
一 山 容 不 下 二 虎：one mountain cannot hold two tigers

比喻一个地方容不得两强共存。

yī tóng shuǐ bù xiǎng bàn tǒng shuǐ huàng dàng
一 桶 水 不 响，半 桶 水 晃 荡。

Proverb: A full bucket of water makes no noise; a bucket half full of water shakes.

Comment: Those who really have knowledge do not give opinions easily. Those with incomplete knowledge are quick to talk.

yī
一：one

tǒng
桶：bucket

shuǐ
水：water

yī tǒng shuǐ
一 桶 水：a full bucket of water

bù
不：no, not

xiǎng
响：a noise

yī tǒng shuǐ bù xiǎng
一 桶 水 不 响：a full bucket of water makes no noise

bàn
半：half

bàn tǒng shuǐ
半 桶 水：bucket half full of water

huàng dàng
晃 荡：shake

bàn tǒng shuǐ huàng dàng
半 桶 水 晃 荡：a bucket half full of water shakes

一桶：比喻知识丰富。半桶：比喻所知不多。响是指炫耀。比喻有真才实学的人不爱自吹自播，不轻易发表意见。一知半解的人却喜欢到处卖弄，自我吹嘘，夸夸其谈。

yí wèi yǔ ér chóu móu wù lín kě ér jué jǐng
宜未雨而绸缪，勿临渴而掘井。

Proverb: Tie up the doors and windows before it rains; do not wait until you are thirsty to dig a well.

Comment: Do not start work at the last moment.

yí
宜：should

wèi
未：not yet

yǔ
雨：rain

wèi yǔ
未雨：not rain yet

ér
而：and then

chóu móu
绸缪：sentimentally attached; here means to tie up the doors or windows

yí wèi yǔ ér chóu móu
宜未雨而绸缪：tie up the doors and windows before it rains

wù
勿：do not, must not

lín
临：when

kě
渴：thirsty

jué
掘：dig

jǐng
井：a well

wù lín kě ér jué jǐng
勿临渴而掘井：do not wait until you are thirsty to dig a well

绸缪：紧密缠缚。最好在下雨之前就把门窗修补好，不要因为口渴再想到去掘井。指做事要先有准备，不要等事到临头才动手。

yǐ	xiǎo	rén	zhī	xīn	dù	jūn	zǐ	zhī	fú
以	小	人	之	心，	度	君	子	之	腹。

Proverb: Small people use their little minds to guess what gentlemen think.

Comment: People say this to put other people down.

yǐ
以：based on, use

xiǎo
小：small

rén
人：people

xiǎo rén
小 人：small people

zhī
之：'s

xīn
心：heart; here means a mind

yǐ xiǎo rén zhī xīn
以 小 人 之 心：small people use their little minds

dù héng liáng
度 = 衡 量：measure; here means guess

jūn zǐ
君 子：a gentleman

fú
腹：a belly; here means a gentleman's thinking

dù jūn zǐ zhī fú
度 君 子 之 腹：guess what gentlemen think

用小人卑劣的想法去猜测道德品行高尚的人的心意。

yǐn shuǐ bú wàng jué jǐng rén
饮 水 不 忘 掘 井 人。

Proverb: When you drink water, don't forget about the people who dug the well.
Comment: The younger generation should not forget what their parents did for them.

yǐn
饮：drink

shuǐ
水：water

bú
不：no, not

wàng wàng jì
忘 = 忘 记：forgete

yǐn shuǐ bú wàng
饮 水 不 忘：when drink water, don't forget

jué wā jué
掘 = 挖 掘：dig

jǐng
井：a well

rén
人：a person, people

juě jǐng rén
掘 井 人：the people who dug the well

指后人不应忘记前人创造出来的幸福。

yīng xióng nán guò měi rén guān
英 雄 难 过 美 人 关。

Proverb: Even heroes cannot resist the temptation of beauty.

Comment: This isn't about art. The heroes are men, beauty refers to women. This is an excuse for men who make mistakes.

yīng xióng
英 雄：a hero; here means a successful man

nán
难：difficult

guò
过：go through; here means resist

nán guò
难 过：difficult to resist

měi
美：beautiful

rén
人：people, a person

měi rén
美 人：beautiful women

guān guān kǎ
关 = 关 卡：the gateway; here means the temptation

yīng xióng nán guò měi rén guān
英 雄 难 过 美 人 关：even heroes can't resist the temptation of beauty

才能出众的英雄人物很难通过美人这一关卡，往往因为迷恋女色而丧失斗志，犯错误或失败。

硬汉难避枕边风

yìng hàn nán bì zhěn biān fēng
硬汉难避枕边风。

Proverb: Even a tough man has a hard time not listening to a woman's pillow talk.

Comment: The heroic or tough man is swayed by a woman's charms.

yìng
硬：strong, tough

hàn
汉：the Han Chinese race

yìng hàn
硬汉：a tough man

nán
难：hard

bì bì kāi
避 = 避开：avoid

nán bì
难避：hard to avoid

zhěn zhěn tou
枕 = 枕头：pillow

biān páng biān
边 = 旁边：nearby

fēng
风：wind

zhěn biān fēng
枕边风：the wind of pillow talk; means a woman's pillow talk

yìng hàn nán bì zhěn biān fēng
硬汉难避枕边风：even a tough man has a hard time not listening to a woman's pillow talk

枕边风：指与男子同床共枕的女人的话。再硬的汉子也难免听信妻子或情妇的话。也指被宠爱的女人在男人面前说话很顶用。

yóu yán bào chǎo bú jìn dē é luǎn shí
油盐爆炒不进的鹅卵石。

Proverb: Cobblestones cannot absorb the flavor of oil and salt by stir-frying.

Comment: Some people cannot be receptive to other people's advice.

yóu
油：oil

yán
盐：salt

bào chǎo
爆炒：stir-fry

bú
不：no, not

jìn
进：enter

bú jìn
不进：cannot absorb

yóu yán bào chǎo bú jìn
油盐爆炒不进：can't absorb the flavor of oil and salt by stir-frying

dē
的：'s

é
鹅：a goose

luǎn
卵：egg

shí
石：stone

é luǎn shí
鹅卵石：cobblestone

yóu yán bào chǎo bú jìn dē é luǎn shí
油盐爆炒不进的鹅卵石：cobblestones cannot absorb the flavor of oil and salt by stir-frying

油盐是烹饪菜肴的调料，鹅卵石根本吸收不了，比喻某些听不进别人规劝的人。

yǒu péng zì yuǎn fāng lái bú yì lè hū
有 朋 自 远 方 来，不 亦 乐 乎。

Proverb: How happy we are to meet a friend who has come from a faraway place.

Comment: This is usually said in social intercourse, to show a joyful feeling.

yǒu
有：have

péng péng yǒu
朋 = 朋 友：friend

zì cóng
自 = 从：from

yuǎn fāng
远 方：a faraway place

lái
来：come

yǒu péng zì yuǎn fāng lái
有 朋 自 远 方 来：have a friend come from a faraway place

bú
不：no, not

yì
亦：also

lè
乐：happy

hū
乎：no meaning, a interjection

bú yì lè hū
不亦乐乎：how happy we are

指有好朋友从远方来，是再快乐不过的事了。常用在应酬场合。

yǒu qián néng shǐ guǐ tuī mò
有 钱 能 使 鬼 推 磨。

Proverb: Money can make a ghost push a millwheel.
Comment: Money can do anything.

yǒu
有：have

qián
钱：money

néng
能：can

shǐ
使：make

guǐ
鬼：a ghost

tuī
推：push

mò
磨：millwheel

guǐ tuī mò
鬼 推 磨：a ghost push a millwheel

yǒu qián néng shǐ guǐ tuī mò
有 钱 能 使 鬼 推 磨：money can make a ghost push a millwheel

旧时认为金钱万能，只要有了钱，什么都能办到，连鬼都可以差遣。

yǒu qiāng jiù shì cǎo tóu wáng
有 枪 就 是 草 头 王。

Proverb: The man with the gun is the local king.

Comment: Chairman Mao said all power flows from the barrel of a gun. He must have been familiar with this proverb.

yǒu
有：have

qiāng
枪：gun

jiù shì
就 是：be sure is

cǎo
草：grass

tóu
头：head

wáng huáng dì
王 = 皇 帝：king, emperor

cǎo tóu wáng
草 头 王：local king

yǒu qiāng jiù shì cǎo tóu wáng
有 枪 就 是 草 头 王：the man with the gun is the local king

草头王：草根族，民间的土皇帝。指谁掌握了枪杆子，就可以称霸一方。

yǒu yǎn bú shì tài shān
有 眼 不 识 泰 山。

Proverb: A person has eyes but cannot recognize Tai Shan mountain.
Comment: Tai Shan mountain is the biggest mountain in China.
Tai Shan mountain symbolizes VIPs. This proverb pokes fun at people whose limited knowledge prevents them from recognizing VIPs.

yǒu
有：have

yǎn
眼：eye

bú
不：no, not

shì rèn shì
识 = 认 识：recognize

tài shān
泰 山：Tai Shan mountain, the biggest mountain in China

yǒu yǎn bú shì tài shān
有 眼 不识泰 山：has eyes but not recognize the Tai Shan mountain

泰山为全国五大名山之冠。长着眼睛却不认识泰山，比喻见识太浅，认不出地位高的重要人物。

yòu yào mǎ ér pǎo yòu yào mǎ ér bù chī cǎo
又要马儿跑，又要马儿不吃草。

Proverb: One expectation is that the horse runs fast; another is that there is no need to feed the horse.

Comment: Greedy people want to gain extra advantage without paying.

yòu
又：again

yào
要：want; here means expect

mǎ ér = mǎ
马儿 = 马：horse

pǎo
跑：run; here means run fast

yòu yào mǎ ér pǎo
又要马儿跑：one expectation is that the horse runs fast

bù
不：no, not

chī
吃：eat

cǎo
草：grass

bù chī cǎo
不吃草：no need to feed

yòu yào mǎ ér bù chī cǎo
又要马儿不吃草：another is that there is no need to feed the horse

指占便宜的心态，东西要好的，但最好不要多费钱财。也指对他人工作的一种挑剔、刁难。

yòu yào zuò biǎo zi yòu yào lì pái fāng
又要做婊子，又要立牌坊。

Proverb: One woman expects to be a whore, but the other expects to be rewarded with a monumental archway.

Comment: Some people want to do bad things but at the same time leave a good name. In traditional China, a monumental archway was contructed to honor (1) loyality to the emperor, (2) filial obedience to parents, (3) chastity after the death of a husband by not remarrying, and (4) benevolence and righteousness.

yòu
又：again

yào
要：want, wish, expect

zuò
做：become

biǎo zī
婊子：whore

yòu yào zuò biǎo zī
又要做婊子：one woman expects to be a whore

lì jiàn lì
立 = 建立：set up

pái fāng
牌坊：monumental archway

lì pái fāng
立牌坊：constructed a monumental archway

yòu yào lì pái fāng
又要立牌坊：another expects to be rewarded with a monumental archway

牌坊：形状像牌楼的建筑物，旧时用来表彰封建礼教下的忠孝节义人物。忠诚（于君主），孝子（孝顺父母），节妇（守贞节，一辈子只嫁一夫，从一而终），义夫（男子讲仁义）。比喻某人又要做坏事，又要图个好名声。

yú jiàn shí ér bù jiàn gōu rén jiàn lì ér bù jiàn hài
鱼见食而不见钩，人见利而不见害。

Proverb: Fish see the worm but not the hook; people see the benefits but not the harm.

Comment: The explanation is in the proverb and follows the fish metaphor.

yú
鱼：fish

jiàn kàn jiàn
见 = 看 见：see

shí shí wù
食 = 食 物：food

ér
而：it's a link word between two things, here means but

bú
不：no, not

bú jiàn
不 见：not see

gōu
钩：hook

yú jiàn shí ér bú jiàn gōu
鱼见食而不见钩：fish see the worm but not the hook

rén
人：people

lì lì yì
利 = 利 益：benefits

jiàn lì
见 利：see the benefits

hài
害：harm

bú jiàn hài
不 见 害：not see the harm

rén jiàn lì ér bú jiàn hài
人见利而不见害：people see the benefits but not the harm

鱼常是见香饵就吞食，而看不见置它于死地的鱼钩；人常是见利益就谋取，而看不见利益之后有凶险。诫人在利益前面要保持清醒的头脑。

yú zhǎo yú xiā zhǎo xiā wáng bā zhǎo dē shì biē qīn jiā
鱼找鱼，虾找虾，王八找的是鳖亲家。

Proverb: Fish look for fish; shrimp look for shrimp; turtles look for soft-shelled turtles to be their relatives through their children's marriage.
Comment: People always make friends with people like themselves.

yú
鱼：fish

zhǎo
找：look for, find

yú zhǎo yú
鱼 找 鱼：fish look for fish

xiā
虾：shrimp

xiā zhǎo xiā
虾 找 虾：shrimp look for shrimp

wáng bā
王 八：turtles

dē
的：'s

shì
是：is

zhǎo dē shì
找 的 是：look for something

biē
鳖：soft-shelled turtles

qīn jiā
亲 家：relatives through their children's marriage

wáng bā zhǎo dē shì biē qīn jiā
王 八 找 的 是 鳖 亲 家：turtles look for soft-shelled turtles to be their relatives through their children's marriage

人总是找自己同类的人结交。

yù jiā zhī zuì hé huàn wú cí
欲加之罪，何患无词。

Proverb: If I want to make a person guilty, why should I worry about a reason.

Comment: Practical if somewhat cynical advice.

yù
欲：desire, want

jiā
加：add; here means make

zhī
之：'s

zuì
罪：crime, here means guilty

yù jiā zhī zuì
欲加之罪：want to make a person guilty

hé hé yǐ
何 = 何以：how, why

huàn dān xīn
患 = 担心：worry

wú méi yǒu
无 = 没有：not have

cí
词：words; here means a reason

wú cí
无词：no word; here means no reason

hé huàn wú cí
何患无词：why should I worry about a reason

欲：想要。患：担心。辞：说辞，借口。要加害于人，是不愁找不到理由或借口的。指随心所欲地诬陷人。

yù bàng xiāng chí yú rén dé lì
鹬蚌相持，渔人得利。

Proverb: When the snipe and the clam grapple, the fisherman profits.

Comment: A third party benefits from a tussle.

yù
鹬：snipe

bàng
蚌：clam

xiāng chí zhēng chí
相持 = 争持：grapple

yù báng xiāng chí
鹬蚌相持：a snipe and a clam grapple

yú
渔：fish

rén
人：man

yú rén
渔人：fisherman

dé dé dào
得 = 得到：get

lì lì yì
利 = 利益：profit

yú rén dé lì
渔人得利：the fisherman profits

鹬：一种细长嘴的水鸟。相持：争持。鹬和蚌争持难解难分，被捕鱼的人双双捕获。比喻双方相持不下，而使第三者从中得利。

yuǎn lái dē hé shàng huì niàn jīng
远 来 的 和 尚 会 念 经。

Proverb: The monk who comes from far away is better at reciting the scriptures.
Comment: People from another place far away will be more respected than local people.

yuǎn
远：far

lái
来：come

dē
的：'s

yuǎn lái dē
远 来 的：come from far away

hé shàng
和 尚：monk

yuǎn lái dē hé shàng
远 来 的 和 尚：monk who cames from far away

huì
会：can, be good at

niàn
念：recite

jīng jīng wén
经 = 经 文：scripture

niàn jīng
念 经：recite scriptures

huì niàn jīng
会 念 经：better at reciting the scriptures

远来的和尚比本地的更会念经。比喻外来的人比本地人更容易受人尊敬。

zhài duō bù chóu shī duō bù yǎng
债 多 不 愁，虱 多 不 痒。

Proverb: Have too many debts, and you don't worry; have too many lice, and you don't feel an itch.

Comment: After many unfortunate things happen, people get used to them.

zhài
债：debt

duō
多：many, much

zhài duō
债 多：many debts

bù
不：no, not

chóu
愁：worry

bù chóu
不 愁：not worry

zhài duō bù chóu
债 多 不 愁：have too many debts and you don't worry

shī
虱：louse, lice

shī duō
虱 多：many lice

yǎng
痒：itch

bù yǎng
不 痒：not itch

shī duō bù yǎng
虱 多 不 痒：have too many lice and you don't feel an itch

欠债多了，反而不发愁，就像虱子多了反而不觉得痒一样。多指欠债过多，愁也没用，干脆不管它。也指晦气的事情太多，反而习以为常。

zhàn zhē máo kēng bù lā shǐ
占 着 茅 坑 不 拉 屎。

Proverb: Take over a latrine but not to shit.

Comment: This saying is used to describe somebody who takes over a position but does nothing.

zhàn bà zhàn
占 = 霸 占：take over by force

zhē
着：no meaning, indicate action or status is continued

máo kēng
茅 坑：latrine

bù
不：no, not

lā shǐ
拉 屎：shit

zhàn zhē máo kēng bù lā shǐ
占 着 茅 坑 不 拉 屎：take over a latrine but not to shit

形容某些人占着职位不干实事。

zhàn zhē jiè guì zhē tǎo
站着借，跪着讨。

Proverb: You can stand to lend money out; you must kneel to ask for money back.

Comment: Be very cautious when lending money to others.

zhàn
站：stand

zhē
着：no meaning, indicate action or status is continued

jiè
借：lend

zhàn zhē jiè
站 着 借：stand to lend; here means stand to lend money

guì
跪：kneel on the ground

tǎo
讨：ask for somethintg back; here means ask for money back

guì zhē tǎo
跪 着 讨：kneel to ask for money back

站着借给人钱，跪着向人讨还借出去的钱。指借钱给人容易，但讨还钱时却要吃尽苦头。劝人借钱给人时要慎重。

zhēn chā bú jìn shuǐ pō bú jìn
针 插 不 进，水 泼 不 进。

Proverb: A needle can't stick in, and splashed water can't enter.
Comment: This is used to describe an organization or a person who has a closed mind.

zhēn
针：needle

chā
插：stick in

bú
不：no, not

jìn
进：enter

bú jìn
不 进：can't enter

zhēn chā bú jìn
针 插 不 进：a needle can't stick in

shuǐ
水：water

pō
泼：splash

shuǐ pō bú jìn
水 泼 不 进：splashed water can't enter

形容某些组织严密或某些人思想固执，改变不了。

zhī jǐ zhī bǐ bǎi zhàn bú dài
知己知彼，百战不殆。

Proverb: Know yourself and know your enemy; fight hundreds of battles with no danger of defeat.
Comment: If you know yourself and your opponent, you will succeed in life's battles.

zhī zhī dào
知 = 知道：know

jǐ zì jǐ
己 = 自己：oneself

zhī jǐ
知己：know oneself

bǐ
彼：another person; here means enemy

zhī jǐ zhī bǐ
知己知彼：know yourself and know your enemy

bǎi
百：hundred; means many

zhàn zhàn zhēng
战 = 战争：fight, battle

bú
不：no, not

dài wéi xiǎn
殆 = 危险：danger

bǎi zhàn bú dài
百战不殆：fight hundreds of battles with no danger of defeat

在军事纷争中，既了解敌人，又了解自己，百战都不会失败

zhǐ jiàn zéi chī ròu méi jiàn zéi āi dǎ
只 见 贼 吃 肉，没 见 贼 挨 打。

Proverb: Only see the thief eat the meat; do not see the thief suffer from a beating.

Comment: We only see others gain extra advantage. We don't think of how much sacrifice they made to be in the limelight.

zhǐ
只：only

jiàn kàn jiàn
见 = 看 见：see

zhǐ jiàn
只 见：only see

zéi
贼：thief

chī
吃：eat

ròu
肉：meat

zhǐ jiàn zéi chī ròu
只 见 贼 吃 肉：only see the thief eat the meat

méi méi yǒu
没 = 没 有：not have

méi jiàn
没 见：not see

āi
挨：suffer from

dǎ
打：beat

méi jiàn zéi āi dě
没 见 贼 挨 打：not see the thief suffer from a beating

指遇事只看到人家享受或占到便宜，而不去想人家曾经为这些表面风光付出多少。

zhǐ xǔ zhōu guān fàng huǒ bù xǔ bǎi xìng diǎn dēng
只许州官放火，不许百姓点灯。

Proverb: Only state officials are allowed to set a fire; common people are not allowed to light a lamp.

Comment: The law is set up to restrain other people. Do as I say, not as I do.

zhǐ
只：only

xǔ yǔn xǔ
许 = 允许：allow

zhōu
州：state

guān
官：official

zhōu guān
州官：a state official

fàng huǒ
放火：set a fire

zhǐ xǔ zhōu guān fàng huǒ
只许州官放火：only state officials are allowed to set a fire

bù
不：no, not

bù xǔ
不许：not allow

bǎi xìng
百姓：common people

diǎn dēng
点灯：light a lamp

bù xǔ bǎi xìng diǎn dēng
不许百姓点灯：common people are not allowed to light a lamp

指有权势的人自己可以胡作非为，却不许其他人有正当的权利。也指对某些人来说，法律只是用来约束别人的。

zhōng chén bú shì èr jūn liè nǚ bú jià èr fū
忠 臣 不 侍 二 君，烈 女 不 嫁 二 夫。

Proverb: A loyal official cannot serve two emperors; a chaste widow is ready to follow her husband in death and not remarry.
Comment: People say this to show their loyalty to one person.

zhōng
忠：loyal

chén
臣：official

bú
不：no, not

shì shì fèng
侍 = 侍 奉：serve

èr
二：two

jūn jūn zhǔ
君 = 君 主：emperor

zhōng chén bú shì èr jūn
忠 臣 不 侍 二 君：a loyal official cannot serve two emperors

liè xìng gé gāng liè
烈 = 性 格 刚 烈：spirited character

nǚ
女：female

liè nǚ
烈 女：a chaste widow, she is ready to follow her husband in death

jià
嫁：marry

fū zhàng fū
夫 = 丈 夫：husband

èr fū
二 夫：two husbands

liè nǚ bú jià èr fū
烈 女 不 嫁 二 夫：a chaste widow is ready to follow her husband in death and not remarry

忠义的臣子不侍奉别的国君，贞节的女子不嫁第二个丈夫。常用来表明忠诚坚贞，绝无二心。

zhòng shǎng zhī xià bì yǒu yǒng fū
重 赏 之 下 必 有 勇 夫，

xiāng ěr zhī xià bì yǒu sǐ yú
香 饵 之 下 必 有 死 鱼。

Proverb: For a handsome reward, you will be sure to attract a brave man ready to die for it; with sweet-smelling bait, you will be sure to attract fish ready to die for it.

Comment: People will die for money.

zhòng
重：heavy, weight

shǎng shǎng cì
赏 = 赏 赐：award

zhòng shǎng
重 赏：handsome reward; here means big reward

zhī
之：'s

xià
下：under, below

zhī xià
之下：under something

zhòng shǎng zhī xià
重 赏 之 下：under a handsome reward

bì bì dìng
必 = 必 定：be sure

yǒu
有：have

bì yǒu
必 有：be sure to find

yǒng yǒng gǎn
勇 = 勇 敢：brave

fū
夫：man, male

yǒng fū
勇 夫：a brave man

bì yǒu yǒng fū
必 有 勇 夫：be sure to attract a brave man

xiāng
香：fragrant

ěr
饵：bait

xiāng ěr
香 饵：sweet-smelling bait

xiāng ěr zhī xià
香 饵 之 下：with sweet-smelling bait

sǐ
死：die

yú
鱼：fish

sǐ yú
死 鱼：dead fish

bì yǒu sǐ yú
必 有 死 鱼：will be sure to find a dead fish

只要重金悬赏，就会出现拿生命去冒险的奋勇之人，正像鱼因为贪吃美味的鱼饵而丧命一样。

zhòng guā dé guā zhòng dòu dé dòu
种 瓜 得 瓜，种 豆 得 豆。

Proverb: Plant melons, harvest melons; plant beans, harvest beans.

Comment: This proverb tells people that what you pay for is what you get.

zhòng
种：plant

guā
瓜：melon

zhòng guā
种 瓜：plant melons

dé dé dào
得 = 得 到：get, gain

dé guā
得 瓜：harvest melons

zhòng guā dé guā
种 瓜 得 瓜：plant melons, harvest melons

dòu
豆：beans

zhòng dòu
种 豆：plant beans

dé dòu
得 豆：harvest beans

zhòng dòu dé dòu
种 豆 得 豆：plant beans, harvest beans

种什么就能收获什么。因果关系，指做了什么事情就会得到什么样的结果。

zhú lán dǎ shuǐ yī chǎng kōng
竹 篮 打 水 一 场 空。

Proverb: Use a bamboo basket to scoop up water, and it comes up empty.
Comment: Work stupidly, achieve nothing.

zhú
竹：bamboo

lán lán zi
篮 = 篮 子：basket

zhú lán
竹 篮：a bamboo basket

dǎ
打：hit, beat

shuǐ
水：water

dǎ shuǐ
打 水：pick up water

yī
一：one

chǎng
场：a measure word for action

kōng
空：empty

yī chǎng kōng
一 场 空：comes up empty

zhú lán dǎ shuǐ yī chǎng kōng
竹 篮 打 水 一 场 空：use a bamboo basket to scoop up water and it comes up empty

用竹篮打水，水很快就漏光了。比喻白费力气，劳而无功。

zhǔ shóu dē yā zi yòu fēi le
煮 熟 的 鸭 子 又 飞 了。

Proverb: A cooked duck flies out again.
Comment: This refers to something that looks like a big success in the beginning and then later turns out to be a failure.

zhǔ
煮：cook

shóu
熟：ripe

dē
的：'s

yā zi
鸭 子：duck

zhǔ shóu dē yā zi
煮 熟 的 鸭 子：a cooked duck

yòu
又：again

fēi
飞：fly

le
了：no meaning, used after adjective to show change already finished

yòu fēi le
又 飞 了：fly out again

形容本来已经非常有把握或差不多要办成的事情，结果又没办成。

zhuō zéi zhuō zāng zhuō jiān zhuō shuāng
捉 贼 捉 赃，捉 奸 捉 双。

Proverb: If you catch a thief, you must recover the stolen goods; if you catch adulterers, you must catch them both.

Comment: To decide a case, you should have conclusive evidence.

zhuō
捉：catch

zéi
贼：thief

zāng zāng wù
赃 = 赃 物：stolen goods

zhuō zāng
捉 赃：catch stolen goods; means recover the stolen goods

zhuō zéi zhuō zāng
捉 贼 捉 赃：catch a thief, you must recover the stolen goods

jiān
奸：adulterers

zhuō jiān
捉 奸：catch adulterers

shuāng
双：both, a pair

zhuō shuāng
捉 双：catch both

zhuō jiān zhuō shuāng
捉 奸 捉 双：catch adulterers, you should catch them both

抓住贼人必须截获赃物，捉奸必须捉住双方。指判定案件，必须要有真凭实据。

zì gǔ hóng yán duō bó mìng
自古红颜多薄命。

Proverb: From ancient times, the majority of beautiful women have had short lives.

Comment: Underlying this saying is the belief that beautiful women are more frequently the object of men's passions and therefore are subject to more troubles and hurt.

zì = zì cóng
自 = 自从：from, since

gǔ
古：ancient, very old

zì gǔ
自古：from ancient times

hóng
红：red

yán = yán miàn
颜 = 颜面：face

hóng yán
红颜：a beautiful woman

duō
多：many, much

bó
薄：thin

mìng = mìng yùn
命 = 命运：fate

bó mìng
薄命：short-lived

zì gǔ hóng yán duō bó mìng
自古红颜多薄命：from ancient times, the majority of beautiful women have had short lives

红颜：指漂亮的女人。指美貌女子的命运大多不幸。

zuò rú zhōng zhàn rú sōng wò rú gōng xíng rú fēng
坐如钟，站如松，卧如弓，行如风。

Proverb: Sit like a clock, stand like a pine tree, sleep like a bow, walk like the wind.
Comment: This saying is an instruction for manners for young people.

zuò
坐：sit

rú
如：as, like

zhōng
钟：clock

zuò rú zhōng
坐 如 钟：sit like a clock

zhàn
站：stand

sōng sōng shù
松 = 松 树：pine tree

zhàn rú sōng
站 如 松：stand like a pine tree

wò
卧 ：sleep

gōng
弓：bow; here means bow-shaped

wò rú gōng
卧 如 弓：sleep like a bow

xíng xíng zǒu
行 = 行 走：twalk

fēng
风：wind

xíng rú fēng
行 如 风：walk like the wind

指人的坐、站、卧、行的四种姿势。坐像钟一样正，站像松一样直，卧像弓一样弯，走路像一阵风。

zuò ruò zhě bù dé hǎo huó zuò qiáng zhě bù dé hǎo sǐ
做弱者不得好活，做强者不得好死。

Proverb: A loser cannot have a comfortable life; a dictator cannot have a good way to die.

Comment: Two incisive messages that are juxtaposed in one proverb.

zuò
做：be

ruò
弱：weak

zhě
者：people, a person

zuò ruò zhě
做 弱 者：be a loser

bù
不：no, not

dé　dé dào
得 = 得 到：get

hǎo
好：good, fine

huó
活：live

hǎo huó
好 活：have a comfortable life

zuò ruò zhě bù dé hǎo huó
做 弱 者 不 得 好 活：a loser cannot have a comfortable life

qiáng
强：strong, powerful

zuò qiáng zhě
做 强 者：be a dictator

sǐ
死：die

hǎo sǐ
好 死：good way to die

zuò qiáng zhě bù dé hǎo sǐ
做 强 者 不得 好死：a dictator cannot have a good way to die

做弱者或是做强者实际上活得都很辛苦，只是形式不一样。

Track Sequence / each track is for 5 proverbs

Track 01: pg.022—pg.026
Track 02: pg.027—pg.032
Track 03: pg.033—pg.037
Track 04: pg.038—pg.042
Track 05: pg.043—pg.049
Track 06: pg.050—pg.055
Track 07: pg.056—pg.061
Track 08: pg.062—pg.068
Track 09: pg.069—pg.074
Track 10: pg.075—pg.079
Track 11: pg.080—pg.085
Track 12: pg.086—pg.091
Track 13: pg.092—pg.096
Track 14: pg.097—pg.102
Track 15: pg.103—pg.107
Track 16: pg.108—pg.112
Track 17: pg.113—pg.118
Track 18: pg.119—pg.123
Track 19: pg.124—pg.128
Track 20: pg.129—pg.133
Track 21: pg.134—pg.138
Track 22: pg.139—pg.143
Track 23: pg.144—pg.148
Track 24: pg.149—pg.153
Track 25: pg.154—pg.158
Track 26: pg.159—pg.163
Track 27: pg.164—pg.168
Track 28: pg.169—pg.174
Track 29: pg.175—pg.179
Track 30: pg.180—pg.185
Track 31: pg.186—pg.190
Track 32: pg.191—pg.195
Track 33: pg.196—pg.200
Track 34: pg.201—pg.205
Track 35: pg.206—pg.211
Track 36: pg.212—pg.216
Track 37: pg.217—pg.223
Track 38: pg.224—pg.228
Track 39: pg.229—pg.233
Track 40: pg.234—pg.239
Track 41: pg.240—pg.245
Track 42: pg.246—pg.251
Track 43: pg.252—pg.257
Track 44: pg.258—pg.263
Track 45: pg.264—pg.268
Track 46: pg.269—pg.273
Track 47: pg.274—pg.280
Track 48: pg.281—pg.285
Track 49: pg.286—pg.291
Track 50: pg.292—pg.297
Track 51: pg.298—pg.304
Track 52: pg.305—pg.310
Track 53: pg.311—pg.315
Track 54: pg.316—pg.320
Track 55: pg.321—pg.326
Track 56: pg.327—pg.331
Track 57: pg.332—pg.336
Track 58: pg.337—pg.341
Track 59: pg.342—pg.347
Track 60: pg.348—pg.352